Alternative Health Care for Children

*Strategies to protect your children from illness, with detailed
information about all the different types of treatment*

Alternative Health Care for Children

A comprehensive guide for parents

by

Eveline de Jong

THORSONS PUBLISHING GROUP

First published in 1989

British Library Cataloguing in
Publication Data

de Jong, Eveline D, *1948-*
    Alternative health care for children:
    a comprehensive guide for parents
    1. Children. Health
    I. Title
    613'0432

    ISBN 0-7225-1553-7

Illustrations by Jane Bottomley

Published by Thorsons Publishers Limited,
Wellingborough, Northamptonshire,
NN8 2RQ, England

Typeset by Harper Phototypesetters Ltd.,
Northampton, England
Printed in Great Britain by
Makays of Chatham, Kent

10 9 8 7 6 5 4 3 2 1

Contents

Acknowledgements

Firstly my thanks go to the many practitioners of alternative therapies who contributed so generously to this book. I am equally grateful to all the parents who shared their experiences with me — in particular the supportive group of parents at Fleet Primary School. Without them I could never have written this book and while I tried to incorporate all their various viewpoints, any errors or omissions are, of course, mine.

My special thanks go to Luke Zander who, very early on, encouraged me to pursue the subject, to Ann Tinklepaugh, who read early drafts of the book, to Angelika Schimmelschmidt, who supplied me with some specific pieces of background information, and to my Alexander teacher Katya Benjamin, who greatly helped me to keep my inner balance during the hectic months of research and writing.

Finally, my gratitude goes to Jan Magnus for support and patience and to Gideon and Hedda for being, among other things, a continuous source of wonder and inspiration.

Introduction

There is a growing interest in and demand for alternative forms of health care. As more and more people are finding that orthodox medicine doesn't hold all the answers to many of their health problems, they begin to explore alternative forms of medicine. However even those parents who use alternative therapies for themselves with confidence often wonder whether these therapies are also suitable for their *children*.

One reason why parents feel apprehensive about seeking alternative treatment for their children is that it is often thought that there is an element of risk attached to using an alternative therapy. While patients usually feel that they can take this risk as long as it concerns only themselves, parents feel far more doubtful when such a treatment would concern their child.

Another reason why parents may hesitate to consult practitioners of alternative forms of medicine for their children is that the image commonly presented to the general public by alternative or complementary medicine is

one of a world 'for adults only'. In alternative medicine a lot of emphasis is put on taking responsibility for your own health, on self-help, and on the relationship between mind and body — areas that all seem very much to belong to the adult world.

With children, the parents look after their offspring's physical and emotional needs. As a matter of fact, many people only begin to be more interested in health care once they have become parents themselves. If, formerly, they might have completely relied on their doctor and accepted without much questioning any form of treatment, as parents they have to become active participants in the actual administration of health care: from the moment a child is born onwards — or rather beginning with antenatal care — parents are responsible for their child's health, they have to care for their child when he or she falls ill and they have to look after their child's physical and emotional needs.

New parents need a lot of information on how to look after their child and we can see this need reflected in the abundance of books on baby and child care. These books usually cover a wide range of subjects, advising parents on medical, psychological, and emotional problems concerning babies and children, but the information is almost always based on orthodox medical knowledge and parents who wonder if there are alternative ways of looking after their children's health will not find an answer to their questions in them. However, more and more parents are, in fact, either contemplating or already using alternative forms of health care for their children. This book gives an overview of current practice of and thinking on alternative health care for children, information about which is at present mainly to be found in small pamphlets and isolated paragraphs in books on alternative

therapies. It also contains information based on interviews with alternative therapists who are particularly interested in and have experience working with children. Last, but not least, it draws upon the experiences of parents themselves, for, although parents are usually urged to take professional advice on matters of health care, I believe that parents can learn a great deal from each other.

Orthodox medicine has its own special branch of paediatrics, which concerns itself with children's illnesses. However, there is not yet its equivalent in alternative medicine. By describing the possibilities and limitations of alternative forms of health care for children, this book also hopes to promote discussion on the subject amongst alternative practitioners themselves.

PART ONE

Preventive health care

CHAPTER ONE

Childbirth

Preconceptual care

Most of us agree that care for your child should begin as early in pregnancy as possible. In practice this will mean that as soon as a woman knows she is pregnant she will be involved in antenatal care. However, care for your child before you are even pregnant? Isn't this taking things a bit too far? Yet, this is precisely what is promoted by Foresight, the Association For the Promotion of Pre-conceptual Care. Based on the belief that healthier parents may conceive healthier babies, they argue that care for your child should begin before even having conceived it.

With the advances made in contraceptives and the resulting increase in planned pregnancies, the aims of Foresight just seem one logical step further: if you plan your pregnancy, you might as well plan to conceive your child in an optimum biological mini environment — in this case two healthy parents.

Foresight has drawn up a list of recommendations as to how parents can prepare themselves. Some of these recommendations are quite straightforward, such as stop smoking and drinking, and eat a healthy diet. They also recommend that you stop taking the pill or using the copper coil at least four to six months before planning to conceive. In addition, they recommend a full analysis of the health of both parents after which steps can be taken to correct any deficiencies.

In Great Britain, the association has created a network of clinicians (doctors in private practice) who will carry out a number of tests according to the 'Foresight Clinic Protocol' for parents interested in preconceptual care. These tests include blood pressure, rubella status, basal temperature, urine analysis, blood examination, hair analysis (to assess concentrations of essential and toxic metals), smear test, stool samples, and semen samples. Some of these tests are part of the usual examination of women who are pregnant, while other tests are reserved for those couples who have difficulty in conceiving. Similarly, the recommendations concerning a healthy lifestyle and diet are also part of general prenatal advice. Foresight urges parents to stop and think *before* conception, rather than wait until after, when, it is argued, some factors may have already had an effect on the unborn child.

Further information

Foresight, The Association For the Promotion of Pre-Conceptual Care, The Old Vicarage, Church Lane, Witley, Godalming, Surrey, GU8 5PN (tel: 042879 4500).

Getting in touch with your unborn child

It is possible to get in touch with your unborn child and, if so, how do you go about it?

There are now advanced and complicated machines to register the unborn baby's heartbeat and to monitor its growth on a regular basis. For every mother-to-be it is exciting to hear her baby's heartbeat through a loudspeaker or to see the baby move around on a screen, but, at home, without the use of complicated instruments, it is also perfectly possible to get to know your child before it is born, by touching it, caressing it, playing with it.

Every pregnant woman knows how it feels when her baby moves around inside her and enjoys these positive signs of life, but, rather than passively enjoying your baby's movements, you can as a mother, and as a father as well, actively get involved in touching the baby and responding to its movements.

One way in which parents can notice that their child responds to their touch is by taking a fixed time in the day, say early in the morning or before going to bed, to play with their child. Soon they will notice that the child anticipates this special

moment by responding immediately to the parents' hands on the mother's tummy.

The unborn child reacts to the touching of its parents by movement. The way it moves, can express that it wants more contact or less. The baby will try to follow a soft touch or caress, it will try to evade a sudden or harsh touch. By taking this time and exploring through touch, you can already get to know your child before it is born, and, just as important, your child can get to know you.

Apart from being sensitive to touch, your unborn child can also hear sounds from outside the womb. Not only can it hear its mother's voice, but it will learn to recognize the father's voice as well. So, as well as touching your unborn child, you can also talk to it.

In the same way that early postnatal bonding, or extra-uterine bonding as it is sometimes called, has become recognized as an important and essential part of the early development of a child, bonding that takes place before birth, or intra-uterine bonding is increasingly recognized as being important too. The best time for this active bonding to take place is thought to be the last three or two months of preg-

nancy, by which time the unborn child is thought to be physically and intellectually mature enough to send and receive fairly sophisticated messages.

Parents who are aware of their baby's movements before birth, often see that various patterns of waking, playing and sleeping are sustained after birth. One pattern that many babies display, whether their parents have made an effort to get in touch with them before birth or not, is that they are difficult and fretful between five and seven in the evening — just when the mother is at her busiest, especially when there are older children to look after. Babies don't display this behaviour to make life more difficult for their mother, but because they had this pattern already instilled in them before birth. The mother was always busy during that time of day when she still carried the baby inside her. As a consequence, the baby has come to expect a lot of movement at that time and will react against being left alone in a cot or crib. Research into babies' sleeping habits has also shown that a mother's sleeping habits before the baby is born have an effect on the baby's sleeping patterns after birth: early risers give birth to early-rising babies and late-to-bed mothers have late-to-bed children.

When expecting a baby, a woman often finds herself confronted with a lot of don'ts: do not smoke, do not drink alcohol, do not take medicines, do not lift heavy objects. Getting in touch with her unborn child, however, is something a woman *can* do, and not only because it benefits her child, but because it is a very enjoyable experience for her.

Further information
W. Pollmann-Wardenier, 'Over de haptonomische zwangerschapsbege-leiding', *Verkenningen in de Haptonomie*, W. Pollmann-Wardenier (Ed.) (A.W. Bruna & Zn, Utrecht, 1986)
Thomas Verny (with John Kelly), *The Secret Life of the Unborn Child* (Sphere, 1982)

Where to be born

The great majority of babies in the Western world are born in hospital. The tendency to have babies in hospital was started in the nineteenth century, although in those early days it was generally recognized that infant mortality was much higher for hospital births than for home births. The biggest increase in hospital births and the phasing out of home deliveries, however, didn't take place until after the Second World War.

It is generally thought, by the medical world and prospective parents alike, that hospital is the safest place for a baby to be born. This thought is usually based on the fact that the decline in the mortality rate of babies around the time of birth took place at approximately the same time as the large increase in hospital births. However, recent statistical analysis has shown that this apparent link is not, in fact, the cause and the effect as was previously supposed, and that there is no scientific evidence to show that hospital is indeed the safest place.

The fact that home births have all but disappeared in the Western world — with the notable exception of the Netherlands, where one third of all babies are born at home — is due to a number of political, economical as well as medical reasons. In recent years women have started to question these reasons and have begun a fight to gain back what they have lost: the right to choose where to have their babies. The question is not so much which is the better or safer place to have your baby, but that both hospital *and* home can function as the appropriate place and that each woman should be in a position to make an informed decision as to where she wants her baby to be born.

The right for each woman to choose the type of birth care she prefers is, in fact, one of the recommendations issued by the World Health Organization during the Inter-regional Conference for Birth, held in 1985. Many other of the 15 recommendations strongly advise against unnecessary technological intervention during the birth process and underline the fact that social, emotional and psychological factors are decisive in the understanding and implementation of proper antenatal care.

As was pointed out during the First International Conference on Home Births, held in London in October 1986, the availability of home births is not an isolated issue propagated by a handful of feminist women. It is an illustration of the growing tendency of patients in general to ask for a medical approach that is patient-oriented rather than disease-oriented. It is interesting to note that this request is also thought to be reflected in the growing number of people who seek alternative forms of medical care.

There is as little need for idealizing home birth as there is for denouncing it as being unsafe, for the latter is untrue while the former may give opponents of home birth a chance to ignore the real arguments. What is necessary is to ensure that during childbirth high standards of medical care are combined with a sensitivity to the wishes and needs of mothers and their babies — something that is possible to do in a hospital as well as at home.

Home birth

Women choose to have their baby at home as opposed to a hospital because:

● They want to be somewhere where they truly feel at home and where they can choose the people they want to be present during the delivery such as relatives and friends.

● Being at home allows for more freedom of movement, both during labour and birth, than is usually possible at hospital.

● They can be active participants in the decision-making in all stages of labour and birth instead of being a patient with little or no say in the procedure.

● They can establish a personal relationship with the one midwife or doctor involved instead of the likelihood of dealing with a number of different hospital staff.

● Unnecessary medical intervention can be avoided.

● They want to avoid hospitals as they are associated with illness and death rather than with health and birth.

If you want to consider a home birth for your child, your main problem will probably be to find people who are not only sympathetic to your ideas, but who can help you to carry out your plans. How difficult this will be greatly depends on where you live and it is best to contact a national organization for the promotion of home birth that can help you to get in touch with the people you need.

As the Dutch example shows on a large scale and as small groups of determined women in countries such as Britain and the USA are showing, a planned home birth that takes place after proper screening for risk factors can be a safe and more pleasurable, positive experience for the mother than a delivery in a hospital setting.

What about the baby? Does it benefit from being born either at home or in a hospital? To answer this question, we will try and look at the birth experience from the perspective of the baby being born.

Further information
Rona Campbell and Alison Macfarlane, *Where to Be Born*? The Debate and the Evidence, The National Perinatal Epidemiology Unit, Radcliffe Infirmary, Oxford, 1987
Luke Zander, 'Home Birth — A challenge to the profession', The First International Conference on Home Birth, London, October 1987

Association for Improvements in the Maternity Services, 21 Iver Lane, Iver, Buckinghamshire SL0 9LH (tel: 0753 652781)
International Home Birth Movement, 22 Anson Road, London N7 0RD

The National Childbirth Trust, Alexandra House, Oldham Terrace, London W3 6NH (tel: 01-992 8637)
The International Centre for Active Birth, 55 Dartmouth Park Road, London NW5 1SL (tel: 01-267 3006)

The birth experience

Childbirth involves two people — mother and baby. Concern has always been expressed about both of them — especially their safety and their chances of survival. However, concern about the safety of mother and child doesn't necessarily extend to concern about their physical and emotional well-being.

Childbirth has now become a medical event, needing medically skilled attendants and more and more technical instruments, and often the human aspect of the event tends to get all but lost. People have been forgetting they are dealing with human beings who are going through two of life's major experiences — giving birth and being born. One of the problems with hospital births is that there are so many of them. The birth experience is unique for the mother and child, but for the hospital and its staff, however caring they are, it is a routine event.

Considering the needs of the baby

If, during a routine hospital birth, the needs of mothers in labour have often not always been given the full attention and consideration they deserve, the physical and emotional needs of the baby have been considered even less important. For example, such practices as holding babies upside down by their feet and/or slapping them on their bottoms to make them cry, putting them on cold weighing scales and wrapping or dressing them in tight clothes were and still are common.

Somehow, all those involved in the birth process, professionals as well as parents, need to be reminded of what is really going on. No one reading Frederick Leboyer's book *Birth Without Violence* can fail to be moved by the anguish suffered by the baby during a 'normal' birth and by the peacefulness of a birth attuned to the newborn's needs. Through the text and pictures we are made to realize that newborn babies are sensitive beings who communicate with every means they have at their disposal how they feel about the way they are being treated.

Babies cannot champion their own cause, but mothers can do it for them and, apart from wanting more say in their own experience of giving birth, mothers now also want more consideration for their babies' overall well-being. Everyone has the right to a good start in life and it isn't so very difficult to oblige. The only thing a baby needs is respect and a bit of time: respect for the fact that bright lights, sudden noises, and rough handling must be deeply disturbing when coming from a place where everything was dark and smooth, and time to gradually adjust to the new circumstances while lying on the mother's tummy, the safest place to be when just having come from inside it.

When a child is born at home, all this is quite easy to provide. The room is never as brightly lit as a hospital room, there are only a few people present who will not find it difficult to lower their voices and to be as unobtrusive as possible and, because there are no women in the next room who are giving or have just given birth, there should be no hurry for routines such as weighing and dressing the baby.

No doubt, Leboyer's book has had an immense influence on the way children are being born. Hospitals are now also beginning to change some of their routines and try to make childbirth into a less traumatic experience for both mother and child, although changes in routine practices occur only slowly. It is claimed, however, that the strict 'Leboyer method', which includes immediate skin contact and a bath, is not essential for a less traumatic birth experience and a more responsive baby. A gentle conventional birth that occurs naturally and is drug-free, would be equally effective.

The psychological and emotional aspects of birth

Issues surrounding pregnancy and birth have in recent years begun to attract more attention from the orthodox medical world and the psychological and emotional issues involved in birth for the mother and child in particular are now being studied more extensively. Until recently it was believed that babies are oblivious to whatever happens to them during birth. For, even if babies loudly protest at the time that they don't feel comfortable about what is happening to them, they soon seem to forget and fall asleep. However, it has been argued that babies who are born without too much stress actually stay awake and alert after birth and that babies who fall into a long and deep sleep do so to sleep off the stress of a traumatic birth.

There are also some recent studies that show that birth memories are a reality. Birth produces a kind of amnesic effect, probably because of a hormone secreted by the mother during labour and birth, so that our birth memories slip from conscious recall. However, this doesn't mean that these memories don't survive and stay with us on an *unconscious* level.

A recent study showed that some babies needing an anaesthetic for surgery reacted in a more frantic way to a mask being put on their face than other babies. Through examination of the medical notes made during their birth, it became clear that those babies who had experienced oxygen deprivation during birth, struggled against a mask being put on their face, and a likely explanation is that the mask revived unpleasant memories and the fear of asphyxiation.

In adults, birth memories can be retrieved by hypnosis and one study found that people under hypnosis can even recall how their head and shoulders were positioned during birth.

Therapies such as primal therapy or rebirthing, which use hypnosis to bring a person back to the time of his or her birth with the aim of reliving the birth experience and consequently relieving the trauma, have always postulated that a traumatic birth experience can have long-lasting negative effects on a person. While most accounts of the effects of a traumatic birth are of an anecdotal nature and relate to individuals rather than to groups of people, an American study into suicide among adolescents has now brought to light that among a group of 52 adolescents who committed suicide a larger proportion than usual had experienced respiratory distress for more than one hour at birth.

Whether a child is born at home or at hospital — and there is no one place or one technique that is suitable for everyone — what would seem to matter most is that both mother and child are made to feel physically and emotionally safe. However, while doctors and hospitals in the Western world may begin to heed women's wishes, elsewhere in the world they are only just beginning to follow Western practices and too often it seems that practices are being used that date from the time before they were beginning to be modified, as the following example shows. A recent *Tomorrow's World* programme on television showed a hospital birth in China. Moments after the baby was born, still lying between the mother's legs, a needle was jabbed into the baby's arm (the film extolled the merits of a new vaccination method that was carried out on new-born babies). The next moment the baby was whisked away and weighed. The final picture showed us the mother lying in bed holding a fully dressed baby.

Further information
Frederick Leboyer, *Birth Without Violence* (Fontana, 1977)
Thomas Verny (with John Kelly), *The Secret Life of the Unborn Child* (Sphere, 1982)
John A. Davis, 'The baby's experience', The First International Conference on Home Birth, London, October 1987
Lee Salk, Lewis P. Lipsitt, William Q. Sturner, Bernice M. Reilly, Robin H. Levat, 'Relationship of Maternal and Perinatal Conditions to Eventual Adolescent Suicide', *The Lancet*, 16 March, 1985, pages 624-627

Bonding

It is now more generally recognized that bonding between a mother and her baby should take place, or rather begin, from the moment the baby is born. In more enlightened hospitals and maternity homes, the baby is allowed to lie on the mother's tummy while the two of them are still connected by the umbilical cord or the baby is given to the mother to hold immediately after the birth is complete.

It is argued that proper bonding between the mother and baby ensures a deeper and healthier relationship between mother and child and may also prevent the all too

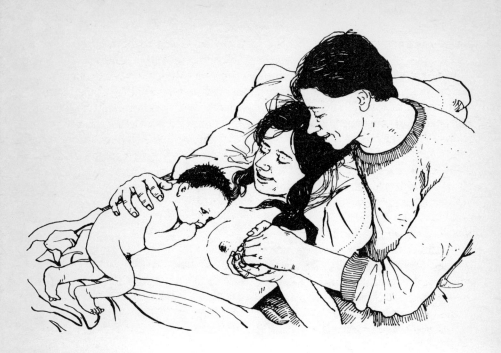

common postpartum depression. One explanation given for this depression is that in humans it is the mother who needs to become imprinted on the baby rather than the baby on her. Unlike many baby animals, who are capable of following their mother around very soon after birth, a human baby is born in a very immature developmental state and is very helpless. To ensure survival for the baby, the mother must feel an overriding urge to take care of the baby and this urge is all the stronger if she is actively involved in the birth process and sees and feels the baby the moment it emerges from her body.

So, the argument continues, if there is no baby to see or hold, either because the mother is too drugged or the baby is taken away from her instantly, the mother's instinctive feeling is that there is no baby because the baby is dead. Even if *consciously* she knows this is not true, the feeling of loss will trigger feelings of mourning in the mother. If then the baby is handed to her some time after the birth, her natural response to want to hold and love her baby is tempered by confused feelings of mourning and loss, and the seeds for depression will have been sown.

However important 'first impressions' are, bonding doesn't stop after one hour or one day after the baby is born. Mother and baby both need time to get to know each other and the more time they spend

Alternative Health Care for Children

Family bonding

Bonding does not just take place in the first hour after birth, nor does it need to be confined to mother and baby. For a father to be present at the birth of his child also helps him to be 'imprinted' on this particular baby. Some would even say that the presence of older brothers and sisters during birth would ensure closer family ties, but for most families this would probably be taking things too far. Also, with today's small families there is often only one older brother or sister around and a two-year-old toddler is not likely to be a very attentive yet unobtrusive audience in the birthing room. But, as is possible when the baby is born at home or in a maternity unit where they allow for this kind of situation, for an older sibling to be allowed into the room and even into the mother's bed as soon as the baby is born, can make the arrival of a new brother or sister a special family affair where everyone involved has a chance to welcome the baby.

housework or by visitors, a mother would benefit from spending as much quiet time as possible with her baby — feeding, resting and sleeping together during the first few weeks. These days, with people living in small rather than extended families, it is often not easy to ensure such a prolonged bonding period for mother and child. Fathers tend to be around a lot more than they used to, but the time they can take off from work is often limited.

In the Netherlands, where home births are still part of the official obstetric practice, there also exists a system whereby home helps come in on a daily basis for ten days after the birth to look after mother and child, to provide meals and to look after older brothers and sisters. To provide such a service is rather beyond what we usually dare to ask a relative or friend, but perhaps friends or relatives would be more willing to oblige than we are inclined to think. To be closely involved with a mother and her new-born baby is a very intimate experience and to be asked to be around, if only for a few days, can be a very special honour.

in each other's company the more they will feel at ease with each other. For, although during the first hours and days of a baby's life, the process of bonding is predominantly a matter of people establishing a relationship with the baby, the baby will soon become an active participant in this process and will begin to respond to the different stimuli offered by its mother and various other people it comes into contact with.

Rather than being overwhelmed by

Further information
Jean Liedloff, *The Continuum Concept* (Penguin, 1986, revised edition)
Natural Childcare, The macrobiotic approach to raising a healthy family (East West Journal Publishing, Massachusetts, 1984)
Marshall H. Klaus and John H. Kennell, *Parent-Infant Bonding*, Second Edition (The C.V. Mosby Company, St Louis, 1982)

The astrological birth chart

One of the things parents may want to consider is having an astrological birth chart or horoscope for their baby. An astrological birth chart is an astronomical map of the solar system depicting the position of the sun, moon, and the other planets at the time of someone's birth. To make such a chart, one needs to know the date, time and place of the birth, to have access to the relevant astronomical tables and to possess some mathematical knowledge to do the necessary calculations.

Once the chart has been made, the more important business of interpreting the chart begins. It is assumed that the particular positions of the sun, moon and their planets and the relationships between them all have a meaning and that, together, they tell something about a person's life.

With the help of one of the many books available these days parents could make a birth chart for their baby themselves, but it is also possible to consult a professional astrologer. Before seeing an astrologer you will have to supply him or her with the time, date and place of your baby's birth, so that the astrologer will be able to prepare a chart before your actual visit. You don't need to take the baby with you when you go to see the astrologer. He or she will explain the meaning of your baby's chart to you, and often the session will be put on tape for you to take home.

How an astrological birth chart can be used

The value or the function of an astrological birth chart is obviously a matter that depends on your own personal tastes and beliefs. It should not be viewed as a firm prediction of your child's future, which would make him or her 'fated' in one

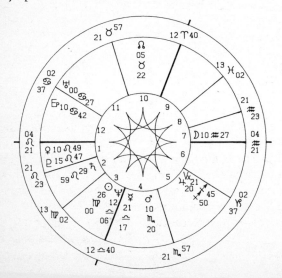

way or another. Rather, it can be seen as a description of someone's strengths and weaknesses, giving someone a choice to use those strengths and to work on their weaknesses.

If parents have a birth chart for their child, it is not something that should be consulted or referred to during every minor upset or event in a child's life, or be used to build up certain expectations. The main thing it should do is to give parents a chance to find out more about their child as a whole person at a time when a child's own means of communicating about himself or herself are still very limited. It could also be consulted if the child should be affected by a particular illness, especially if there are clear psychosomatic overtones.

The chart and the accompanying tape could make a rather special birthday present on, for instance, the child's eighteenth birthday.

Further information
Laurie Efrein, *How to Rectify a Birth Chart*, An introduction to the mathematics of life (The Aquarian Press, 1987)

CHAPTER TWO
Baby care

Life with your baby

Human babies, being born in such an immature developmental state, have to cover an immense range of human development in a very short period of time and it is sometimes put forward that the evolution of human babies is dragging behind the evolution of human beings. When they are born, babies' needs are the same as those of babies born thousands or even millions of years ago, but, almost immediately, they have to begin to adjust to our technologically oriented world or, as Elaine Morgan writes in *The Descent of Woman*, 'What went wrong is that we became civilized; and our babies didn't. We and they belong to areas of human experience removed from one another by millions of years.'

What can we do to bridge all those years? Up till quite recently, to give in to a baby's needs was considered a quick and sure way to spoiling the child. Babies had to learn to adapt to our 'civilized' way of living and the sooner they learned the better. Current thinking has moved away from this principle and has tended to arrive at the opposite conclusion: babies can't be spoilt and mothers should be sensitive to and cater for all their physical and emotional needs by, for example, providing prolonged breast-feeding and continuous physical closeness.

Whatever way you put it — babies have to learn to become civilized as quickly as possible or mothers have to meet all their babies' natural but 'uncivilized' needs — mothers are truly caught in the middle because, even if a mother's first thought is with her baby's needs rather than for the demands of the outside world, her task is still to make her child fit into the modern way of life. Or, as Elaine Morgan continues, 'it is her duty to drag her baby through a few million years of civilization in the course of one short infancy; so that, though she may be the answer to some of her baby's frustrations, she is in fact the source of most of them.'

There is no real solution to this dilemma. Rather, each mother will have to find her own balance in the way she caters for her baby's needs *and* introduces her child to the modern world. However, it has been suggested that, rather than becoming *more* baby-oriented, as prolonged breast-feeding and continuous physical closeness seem to require, mothers should become less baby-oriented. To achieve this, a mother would still breast-feed and sleep with her baby, but do this in such a way that it is incorporated in her life, rather than setting aside special attention and special times for the baby. Or, as Jean Liedloff puts it in *The Continuum Concept*:

> 'It would help immeasurably if we could see baby care as a non-activity. We should learn to regard it as nothing to do. Working, shopping, cooking, cleaning, walking and talking with friends are things to do, to make time for, to think of as activities. The baby (with other children) is simply brought along as a matter of course; no special time need be set aside for him, apart from the minutes devoted to changing nappies. His bath can be part of his mother's. Breast-feeding need not stop all other activity either. It is only a matter of changing one's baby-centred thought patterns to those more suitable for a capable, intelligent being whose nature it is to enjoy work and the companion-ship of other adults.'

By being taken along and thus participating in the mother's life, a baby would learn very quickly about the world, while watching it from a safe place, such as a baby carrier. The smaller amount of undivided attention the baby may receive would be well compensated by the frequent body and eye contact thus provided.

Modern work practices and social life, however, are not geared towards mothers who want to take their babies along wherever they go. Some progress has perhaps been made in recent years, with babies being more acceptable in public places and more public 'mothers' rooms' being available, but women have to continue to make an effort, not only to introduce their babies to our modern world, but also to make the modern world more welcoming to babies.

Further information
Elaine Morgan, *The Descent of Woman*

(Souvenir Press, 1985, revised edition) Jean Liedloff, *The Continuum Concept* (Penguin, 1986)

The Liedloff Continuum Network, P.O. Box 663, London NW1 8XQ

Feeding

Feeding is the most essential part of looking after a baby, but it is also probably the area about which most women, especially first-time mothers, feel most insecure. It is also one of the areas where both fashion and professional advice have changed rather rapidly, especially in the recent past, from breast-feeding to bottle-feeding and back to breast-feeding. Finally, it is an area where commercial interests play a role: there is very little profit to be gained from breast-feeding and all the more from instant formula.

Mothers' insecurity and pressure from the professionals and the commercial world work together to making feeding an endless topic of discussion and so it is not surprising that the longest chapter in almost any book on baby care is on feeding. In baby care books based on orthodox medical knowledge, a lot of space is usually reserved for a discussion of the advantages and disadvantages of bottle-feeding versus breast-feeding. In books that discuss various forms of alternative health care, the assumption is always made that breast-feeding is the best option, as it is invariably considered an important form of preventive health care for both mother and child.

The discussion then centres not on *whether* to breast-feed, but for how long, for although the number of mothers who breast-feed has certainly increased in

recent years, it is not always easy, or convenient, or indeed thought proper, to continue to breast-feed beyond the first few weeks or months.

Women who stop breast-feeding after only a few weeks frequently do so because of lack of information and too little support. If, on turning to their doctors for advice, women find that they are not particularly knowledgeable about breast-feeding and if women do not know about organizations that promote breast-feeding, it is not surprising that they stop or simply give up. It is also argued that one of the reasons why many young mothers today have difficulties breast-feeding is that they were not properly breast-fed themselves, as the upsurge in bottle-feeding and, with it, the decline in breast-feeding took place during the 1950s and 1960s.

Once the initial difficulties have been overcome, however, most women agree that breast-feeding is easy, convenient and cheap compared with bottles. But, after three or four months of easy-going breast-feeding, other obstacles in the form of social life and work begin to loom and no doubt it asks for a new and extra commitment to carry on breast-feeding into the fifth or sixth month and beyond.

Those women who favour breast-feeding beyond the first half year and into the first and even second and third year argue that, although there are some obstacles, there

> *It is said that for those babies who are sucking strongly and therefore successfully early on, nursing becomes increasingly rewarding and they are often the ones who want to go on nursing for longer than other babies who may lose interest as soon as they are introduced to grown-up food and drink. At least, this is what you may notice if you let the baby have a choice. Usually, however, it is the mother who decides when the moment of weaning has arrived and not the child.*

are some clear advantages that, for them, outweigh the disadvantages, such as not being able to go away for any length of time or the general feeling of your body not being your own. One of the advantages frequently mentioned is bed-time nursing, as it helps a child to go to sleep more easily and quickly. Nursing a child at bed-time is therefore often kept up longest, even if a child is completely weaned during the day. Another time when breast-feeding an older baby seems to have a very positive effect is when the child isn't feeling well, as it is often found that breast-fed children recover more quickly from illness.

However, it is only fair to say that breast-feeding in itself, whether it is done for a shorter or a longer period, will not *guarantee* that mother and baby will be healthier, more relaxed and have a close, easy relationship. If breast-feeding makes a mother feel tense and uncomfortable, it will not make her baby relaxed and comfortable and it is even said that a mother's negative feelings about breast-feeding can convey negative emotions

about food that may be carried into later life. But, in the same way that women who choose not to breast-feed should not be made to feel guilty, women who enjoy breast-feeding their children should feel absolutely free to carry on as long as they and their children want to.

Further information
Michel Odent, *Primal Health*, A blueprint for our survival (Century, 1986)
Nursing Beyond One, The National Childbirth Trust, Alexandra House, Oldham Terrace, London W3 6NH (tel: 01-992 8637)
Thomas Verny (with John Kelly), *The Secret Life of the Unborn Child* (Sphere, 1982)
La Leche League International, *The Womanly Art of Breastfeeding*, Fourth Edition (New American Library, New York, 1987)
Association of Breast-feeding Mothers, 131 Mayow Road, London SE26 (tel: 01-778 4769 — telephone counselling service)

The importance of touch

Apart from the need to be fed, a baby's strongest need is probably to be held and to feel motion. Babies don't hear or see or smell very much straight away, but their skin is already a highly developed sensory organ. Babies want to be held, because they want to be touched and they want to feel motion, because that is what they were feeling all the time while still in the mother's womb.

The importance of touch for people of all ages is only slowly beginning to be recognized or rediscovered, after most forms of touching had been given such a sexual connotation that it could almost only take place behind closed doors. However, everyone needs to touch and be touched and, to fulfil this need, it is said that some children will misbehave in order to get spanked, thus be touched, and that teenagers will start having sex at too young an age. Babies and elderly people need touch most of all because their other sensory organs are not yet completely developed or no longer function properly. Elderly people are now sometimes given pets in recognition of this need for tactile experience. Babies have their mothers to touch and hold them. It is argued that, to give babies what they want and need most, they should be carried around during the day and should be allowed to sleep with the mother during the night: in the same way babies are continually with the mother before they are born, they want to be with their mother 24 hours a day during the first months of their lives.

The fact that such 24-hour care can actually be a matter of life and death has been demonstrated by the care given to premature babies in Bogota where, instead of being put in an incubator (too few of which were available anyway), premature babies are being carried around by the mother for 24 hours a day. Since the introduction of this method, the survival rate of premature babies has gone up dramatically.

Sleeping arrangements

All this is a far cry from what is common practice in modern Western society where babies are commonly put down to sleep by themselves during most of the day and, preferably, all through the night. Moreover, non-moving cribs or cots have replaced cradles, which at least ensured a rocking motion, as a more economical solution to a fast growing baby, lasting well into the toddler years.

Nowadays, most women would feel that having a baby with them for 24 hours a day would constitute too big an intrusion into their lives or they would even experience it as a loss of identity as a person in their own right. Babies, however don't particularly care about their mothers' wishes for privacy and they can go on protesting against the sleeping arrangements for a very long time, usually well into their toddler years and beyond.

Sleeping problems among babies and young children are extremely common. It is also one of the most discussed subjects among mothers and during these discussions, many parents will admit that they have 'given in', that a child now spends most nights, or parts of most nights in their bed. This is often a solution to a struggle that may have been going on for quite a long time but, as children get older, their screams become less easy to ignore and, eventually, they will be old enough to leave their own bed and climb into their parents' bed of their own accord.

It is argued that most of these sleeping problems and the struggle they usually involve can be avoided by letting the baby sleep with the mother from the beginning. In *The Family Bed* by Tine Thevenin, a book on small children sleeping with their parents, these and other benefits of families sleeping together are put forward in an eloquent and convincing way, while it is also pointed out that, rather than making the baby or toddler *more* dependent, the feelings of safety and security they get from the experience ensure more sociable and self-reliant children later in life.

Letting your baby sleep with you has also been put forward as a way to prevent cot death, or Sudden Infant Death Syndrome (SIDS), the sudden and unexplained death of a baby between one and seven months of life, for the simple reason that there is no cot. Although this sounds rather too simple, it does run parallel with the proposition that touch plays an important role in the development of postnatal breathing and babies who sleep with their parents undoubtedly receive much more tactile stimulation than babies who sleep in a cot.

It is said that, even if a mother doesn't take to the idea of such continuous closeness with her baby at first, as she provides more bodily contact, her natural instinct will take over and she will actually begin to want more close contact with her baby.

As mentioned earlier, most modern cots or cribs don't provide the rocking motion babies seem to like so much and that often helps them to get to sleep more quickly

> *Apart from rocking a baby in your arms — or taking it for a ride in the pram or the car — a way to provide a 'rocking session' for a baby is to sit with him or her in a rocking chair, a piece of furniture that should be more prominent in a house with young children than it often is. Indeed, it has been argued that the rocking motion provided by rocking chairs is beneficial for people of any age group, as it improves the circulation, promotes easy breathing and discourages lung congestion.*

and even when lying in a motionless cot, babies like to be rocked, which can be done by putting a hand on a baby's bottom or lower spine and gently providing a sideways motion. This subtle swaying will, more often than not, send a baby into a sound sleep in no time. Some children like to be rocked in this way to help them go to sleep throughout their infancy and it was actually one of my own children's preferred way to fall asleep until being six or seven years old.

There is also a theory that if a baby or young child has sleeping problems, one of the reasons might be geopathic stress, which is caused by harmful earth rays. It is believed that natural earth rays which have become distorted before reaching the earth's surface may cause all sorts of illnesses and complaints, and sleeping problems may be one of them. If your baby insits on sleeping at only one end of the cot, or always ends up squashed against the bars or, when older children refuse to sleep in their own beds at all, this may be seen as an indication of geopathic stress. It is said that if, after simply moving the cot or bed across the room, or sometimes moving it to another room, parents see a noticeable improvement in some such sleeping problems, geopathic stress may well have been among the causes. People who subscribe to this theory think that even cot death could be linked with geopathic stress, as an extreme example of the effect of strong, harmful earth radiation.

Further information
Ashley Montagu, *Touching*, The human significance of the skin (Harper and Row, New York, 1986, third edition)
Michel Odent, *Primal Health*, A blueprint for our survival (Century, 1986)
Tine Thevenin, *The Family Bed* (Avery Publishing Group Inc., New Jersey, 1987)
La Leche League International, *The Womanly Art of Breastfeeding*, Fourth Edition (New American Library, New York, 1987)
Joseph Chilton Pearce, *Magical Child* (Bantam Books, Inc., New York, 1980)
Jean Liedloff, *The Continuum Concept* (Penguin, 1986, revised edition)
Rolf Gordon, *Are You Sleeping in a Safe Place?* Dulwich Health Society, 130 Gipsy Hill, London SE19 1PL (tel: 01-670 5883)

Baby massage

If 24-hour baby care, carrying the baby around most of the time and letting it sleep with you, isn't for you, then there is still a way to ensure that your baby receives regular intensive tactile experience — massage.

Baby massage has been practised for centuries in the East, but is a fairly recent introduction in the West. Among the first to introduce baby massage in Western countries was Frederick Leboyer, who saw the need for baby massage as a kind of follow up to his work in relation to child birth (see page 18). He first came across baby massage in India, a country he visited regularly, and his book *Loving Hands* introduced the traditional art of Indian baby massage in the West.

Proponents of baby massage always point out that, apart from being pleasurable and beneficial for the baby, it is a relaxing and rewarding activity for the parents. You can begin to massage your baby very soon after it is born, although opinions seem to vary as to whether or not you have to wait until the new-born's navel is healed. If you start to give your baby a regular massage from the very beginning, he or she will soon get used to it and will even begin to expect it. Once massage has become a regular feature in the lives of both parent and child, you can carry on with it well into the toddler years and beyond (see page 45).

Contrary to what some people believe, massage is not difficult to learn, although it is certainly true that someone will get better at it through practice and experience. Advocates of baby massage suggest that parents begin to practise massage on each other before their baby is being born.

Another way to start before the baby is born is to hold a session on baby massage in an antenatal group. Here, expectant mothers can practise on each other or, if the antenatal group is part of a larger network, mothers of newborns can be invited to come along and demonstrate baby massage on their own babies.

If you wait to introduce massage to your baby until he or she is somewhat older, you may find that from four or five months onwards he or she becomes too mobile to appreciate the massage and you may have to wait until she is about two years old. In the meantime you may like to introduce your baby to baby gymnastics, which is more tailored to babies' need for movement at that stage of their development.

Taoist massage and shiatsu

In many Eastern countries massage was and is a part of everyday life and is considered an important part of preventive medicine. One system of massage that originated in China and which, in recent years, has been introduced in the West is called taoist massage. It is considered a powerful form of massage because it follows the same meridian lines of energy as are used in acupuncture. It can be used for babies as well as adults and, although it can be applied in order to alleviate certain conditions, particularly if they are related to tension and stress, it is mainly used for preventive health care, as a system of 'body maintenance'.

A very similar form of massage, also

using the same points and lines as in acupuncture, originated in Japan and is called shiatsu (see also page 109). It is a traditional system of massage that has been practised in Japan for more than a thousand years and which has recently started to become popular in Western countries. Apart from being used on adults, it is now also being promoted for parents to use with their babies.

Further information
Frederick Leboyer, *Loving Hands*, The traditional Indian art of baby massaging (Knopf Inc., New York, 1976)
Stephen Russell and Yehudi Gordon, *Massage for Life*, A book of taoist massage for babies and parents, London, 1985, available from 156 Hendon Way, London NW2 0NE
Wataru Ohashi with Mary Hoover, *Touch for Love*, Shiatsu for your baby (Ballantine Books, New York, 1985)
Peter Walker, *Baby Relax*, A parent's guide to baby massage and baby gymnastics (Unwin Hyman, 1986)

The vaccination and immunization debate

Some time ago I went to an open evening on complementary health care organized by a local health centre. The evening was very well attended and, after one of the doctors had said a few introductory remarks, people were invited to ask questions. The first few questions all related to adult problems and experiences. Then someone from the audience raised the topic of vaccination against childhood diseases. For the rest of that evening, all the questions asked and all the answers given, either by one of the doctors, or indeed by someone from the audience, focused on the issues surrounding vaccination and immunization.

The orthodox and alternative views

For many people, the use of either orthodox or alternative health care for their children centres mainly on this one issue: should children be vaccinated against the common childhood infections or not? It is also one of the areas where the two approaches are most at odds with each other: orthodox medical care is a strong advocate of vaccination, while practitioners of alternative medical care, especially homoeopaths and anthroposophical doctors, are, on the whole, opposed to it.

The case for vaccination has always been strongly supported by the orthodox medical world and throughout the years it has been able to convince the general public *and* the politicians of the merits and necessity of mass immunization programmes. Although voices have always been raised against it — sometimes for religious reasons but also for medical reasons — the lobby opposing vaccination for specific health care reasons seems only to have gathered an increased momentum in recent years, in line with the growing interest in alternative health care from the side of patients and parents.

Within this existing controversy, parents (and their children) are the ones who are caught in the middle. What should they believe, the arguments put forward by the orthodox medical establishment, arguments that are backed by official government policy and which seem based on scientific evidence that is the hallmark of orthodox medical care? Or the arguments put forward by alternative practitioners, who, on the one hand, refute many of the scientific facts brought forward by the orthodox medical world and, on the other hand, point out the dangers and risks that they believe are inherent in vaccination?

It is important to remember that immunization against childhood illnesses constitutes only part of the use of vaccination and that the orthodox medical world considers the implementation of immunization programmes one of the areas where it has been very successful in the fight against disease. Research is constantly being carried out to develop new vaccines, the most urgent quest now being for a vaccine against AIDS. The rest of this chapter, however, only concerns itself with vaccinations against childhood illnesses as they are currently administered to babies and children.

The arguments

Whether the arguments are put forward by orthodox medical practitioners or by alternative practitioners, the debate for or against vaccination always tends to become

rather emotional. As parents, we might think that this is because it is our children's health that is at stake, but the emotions involved probably have other causes. As mentioned before, the issue of vaccination and immunization is one of the areas where orthodox and alternative forms of medical care are most at odds with each other. The reason for this is that this question is tied up with the basic premises of both orthodox and alternative forms of medical care on the origin of disease and how the human body copes with it (see also Chapter 4).

Although the different philosophies of the two approaches influence the whole way in which orthodox and alternative medical care are applied, the vaccination and immunization debate seems to have become a kind of battleground where the differences in opinion are being fought out most openly.

To put it in a somewhat simplified way, orthodox medical knowledge assumes that all illness is undesirable and should be prevented, that it is outside our control whether or not a disease will occur in a certain person and that we should use vaccinations to ensure immunity against certain diseases. Alternative medical knowledge assumes that childhood illnesses are a necessary and non-threatening part of growing up, that healthy and well-nourished children are likely to be less prone to various infections and can cope better with them if they occur and that naturally acquired immunity against a disease is to be preferred to artificially acquired immunity.

Apart from having a difference of

opinion based on differing philosophies, both the orthodox and the alternative medical world back their case either for or against vaccination with statistics. The pro-vaccination lobby uses statistics to demonstrate that vaccination has dramatically brought down the number of cases of such illnesses as polio, measles and whooping cough and, with it, the mortality rate. The anti-vaccination lobby uses statistics to show that the mortality rate linked with childhood diseases was already going down in a significant way before the vaccination programmes were instituted.

What both sides agree upon is that vaccinations can carry certain risks. However, they don't agree on the kind and severity of the risks involved. Those against vaccination — and they include some orthodox medical doctors — claim that vaccination carries potential short-term risks, ranging from fever and local skin effects such as swelling and redness to brain damage and even cot death, and long-term risks such as allergies and chronic disease in later life. Those in favour of immunization claim that the risks of vaccinations are considerably smaller than the risks of the diseases they prevent and that with proper screening for contra-indications — so that no child is vaccinated for whom vaccinations would carry a risk — the risks involved for those who are vaccinated are minimal.

Finally, there are doubts about the effectiveness of vaccination, particularly in the case of whooping cough, as it is seen that children may still contract the disease even after having been immunized. It is also argued that in the case of German measles (rubella) the immunity aquired through having had the disease is always permanent, while the immunity derived from vaccination may wear off within only a few years, thus leaving women exposed to the risk of contracting the disease while they are pregnant.

Parents' choices and responsibilities

Meanwhile, parents are faced with the decision whether or not to let their children be vaccinated and there are many parents who feel it is among the most difficult decisions they have to make early in their child's life.

Nowadays, the orthodox medical world recognizes the doubts parents may have about immunization and the official advice is to talk to your GP about it. However, as members of the orthodox medical world, the great majority of GPs are in favour of immunizing children and the most a GP will do is to try and take your doubts away, to tell you about the medically recognized contra-indications and to make sure that they do not apply to your child.

If, as a parent, you want to hear the other side of the immunization and vaccination debate, you may consider consulting a practitioner of alternative health care, in particular a homoeopath or an anthroposophical doctor. Whoever parents consult, orthodox or alternative practitioners or both, they should all just give their opinion and leave the final decision to the parents and, whatever decision the parents make, no one should make them feel guilty about their choice but respect it.

The main thing to realize is that, unless vaccination is legally compulsory, parents have a choice and should exercise their right to choose. Not only can parents decide not to have their child vaccinated, but it is also perfectly possible to opt for certain vaccinations and leave out others, to have them administered in sequence rather than all at once or to have them administered at different time intervals from the usual ones. Not accepting the usual 'cocktail' on offer at a specified time, may mean that parents have to make the effort of making an individual appointment and sometimes getting their own vaccine from a pharmacist, but this should not deter them from making this choice. For the providers of health care, vaccination

---

Making up your mind

It is most important that parents make a choice they can live with, for, either way, whether or not a child is vaccinated, parents will carry the final responsibility for their children's health. If parents decide not to have their child immunized, they are responsible for keeping their child as healthy as possible so that he or she can withstand infections and cope better with them if they occur. However, parents who have their children immunized also have a duty to try and maintain optimum health in their children in order for them to be better protected against possible side-effects of the vaccines themselves.

---

is a routine business administered to masses of people. However, parents have the right and the responsibility to demand to be treated on an individual basis.

Conclusion

Clearly, there are no easy answers in the existing controversy about vaccination and immunization. It is to be expected that immunization will remain among the standard procedures of orthodox medical practice for an as yet undefined period of time. However, changes in practice have occurred in the past and they may well occur in the future.

Other than expressing their doubts and worries and asking for more research to be carried out into the short-term and long-term consequences of vaccinations, there is little parents can contribute in the present debate. The one positive contribution parents can make, however, is, rather than to expect and accept mass immunization programmes, to insist on individual treatment in which the advantages and disadvantages of immunization are being weighed up for individual children. Treatment on a more individual basis may imply an extension of the existing list of contra-indications. It would also imply that more research would have to be carried out into alternative ways of stimulating immunity in children, in particular for those children who are thought to be at risk from vaccination.

Further information
Leon Chaitow, *Vaccination and Immunization: Dangers, Delusions and Alternatives*, What every parent should

know (The C.W. Daniel Company, 1987) Robert S. Mendelsohn, 'The Medical Time Bomb of Immunization against Disease', East West Journal, November 1984, pages 46-52

CHAPTER THREE

The growing child

Food

During baby clinics as well as in books on baby care, mothers of young babies are given a lot of advice on how to feed their offspring, but when a baby has begun to eat solids and starts to join in with the rest of the family, a mother is usually left to her own devices with respect to providing proper food for her child. It seems as if the assumption is made that, although mothers don't know how to feed their *babies*, they all know how to feed their *families*.

If feeding a baby properly and sufficiently is often thought of as a difficult and worrying business, the anxieties and worries probably intensify rather than diminish when it comes to providing a healthy diet for growing children. For, even if parents are committed to raising their children on a healthy diet, it is by no means an easy task to bring up children to eat healthily in a world of snacks, soft drinks and junk food.

One reason why it is so difficult for parents to provide their children with a balanced diet, is that, as a childs gets older, the provision of food takes place more and more outside the parents' control. For a baby, the mother, or other carer of the child, is usually the sole provider of food, but often this changes rather early on in a child's life. As soon as a child is completely fed on solids and is able to digest a variety of foods, eating will become part of the child's social life and this aspect will be almost as important as eating for nourishment.

In a research project investigating mothers' attitudes and practices with respect to their task of providing health care for their young children, it was found that, during an average weekday, a quarter of a group of 135 under-threes had a meal at a relative's, friend's or minder's house and that ten per cent had a meal at home that was attended by someone from outside the household. When so many under-*threes* already have meals outside the family, this percentage must increase as children get older.

Food that is consumed in a social context or which is provided as a snack rather than a meal, is often not as healthy and balanced as food that is provided as a main meal in a family setting. There is ample evidence that the traditional home-cooked family meal is threatening to become a thing of the past. There are many factors contributing to this change: mothers who have jobs, the availability of convenience food and junk food, advertising campaigns and last, but not least, children's preferences.

Food that is directed at children by the commercial world, and which children often tend to prefer, is likely to be highly processed, and usually contains a lot of sugar and fat and even more artificial additives than food for adults. There is mounting evidence, however, that it matters very much what children eat — not only because children need a healthy and wholesome diet containing sufficient vitamins and minerals for their physical development, but because many conditions, including allergies, hyper-activity, and tooth decay, have been linked to artificial additives and the nutritional deficiencies of many processed foods. Together with a sharp increse in obesity in children, the rise in diet-linked con-ditions make us witness these days the phenomenon of malnutrition through overconsumption as opposed to malnutri-tion through underconsumption, which was a contributary cause for many child-hood diseases in the past and still is a cause of childhood illnesses in many parts of the world.

Moreover, there is now also new research that points to a link between food and children's intellectual development. A group of children who were given a vitamin and mineral supplement during an eight month period did better on some intelligence tests than another group of children who were matched for age, sex, school performance and home back-ground, and who were given either a placebo or nothing at all.

Vitamin supplements, however, are not the only solution and it has been pointed out by the British Dietetic Association that a poor diet cannot be made into a balanced diet purely by adding vitamin supplements. In fact, parents are even warned that they could harm their children by giving them overdoses of vitamins, especially of vitamins A, D and B_6, which can be toxic when taken in excess.

As has always been propagated by practitioners of alternative therapies, with their emphasis on preventive health care, and is increasingly being promoted by the orthodox medical world, including the dental profession, the best way to ensure that children get sufficient amounts of vitamins and minerals is to give them a healthy and balanced diet.

Eating healthily

These days, with the growing interest in general fitness and health, there is no shortage of information on what constitutes a healthy and balanced diet for adults and children alike. What seems more difficult to come by, however, is advice for parents on how to implement such a diet without making the provision of food into the battleground it can so easily become.

One way some parents succeed in making their children appreciate healthy and wholesome food is by setting the example themselves. As far as their preferences and dislikes are concerned, most children tend to model themselves on their parents and the way children regard food is no exception to this. Eating habits, both the type of food and the way it is consumed, are very much a family affair. Children who see their parents valuing wholesome food, taking time to prepare it and enjoying sitting down for a meal, are likely to be more inclined to appreciate good food than children whose parents themselves mostly consume poor-quality food that is eaten as a snack rather than a proper meal.

Even if parents and children enjoy eating healthy meals together on a regular basis, however, there are also many occasions when parents don't provide their children's meals. School lunches, eating at friends' houses and parties are all frequent occasions when children don't eat at home. However, parents can still teach their children as they grow older to avoid junk food as much as possible, to read food labels and to avoid artificial flavours and colours and to drink fruit juice instead of soft drinks. Some parents now think that making their children aware of what constitutes wholesome food is as important and natural as teaching them to wash their hands and clean their teeth.

While there are many occasions when parents do not provide the food their children eat, breakfast is still the one meal that is usually eaten at home. This gives parents an excellent opportunity to have their children eat a balanced and proper meal: Rather than quickly grabbing a piece of toast or not eating anything at all, parents and children can make breakfast into a meal where a sufficient amount of essential foodstuffs is being consumed. Someone who eats a nutritious breakfast has a sufficient amount of energy for the first half of the day and has less need for sugary snacks before lunch.

To have enough appetite to eat a full breakfast, the last meal of the day should not be too heavy. As you don't need as much energy for sleeping at night as you do for working in the morning, it seems rather odd that dinner is often a far more substantial meal than breakfast, instead of the other way round. This tendency 'to eat backwards' (eat more as one needs to do less) is very common, although it is not necessarily the most healthy or logical way to go about it and it is contrary to an old saying that goes: 'eat like a king for breakfast, like a lord for lunch and dine like a pauper for supper'.

Guidelines for eating healthily away from home

What sort of rules of thumb might help guide a growing child through the hundreds of options in school canteens, snack bars and other places where they can buy prepared food? Martin Lorin (see right) offers some suggestions:

● Don't eat the same junk foods each day

● Try to avoid artificial flavours and colours

● If there isn't a choice of some decent food, eat less now and more later at home

● Instead of a can of fizzy drink, try juice, skimmed milk or mineral water

● Instead of white bread, choose wholemeal, granary or rye and use margarine instead of butter

● Instead of ice-cream, try sorbets or frozen yogurts

● Choose fruit or low-fat yogurt for dessert instead of cake or pie

● If any item tastes bad, leave it.

Further information

Berry Mayall, *Keeping Children Healthy*, The role of mothers and professionals (Allen & Unwin, 1986)

Belinda Barnes and Irene Colquhoun, *The Hyperactive Child* (Thorsons, 1984)

David Benton and Gwilym Roberts, 'Effect of Vitamin and Mineral Supplementation on Intelligence of a Sample of Schoolchildren', *The Lancet*, January 23, 1988, pages 140-143

Brian Halvorsen, *The Natural Dentist*, A holistic approach to the prevention of dental disease (Century Hutchinson, 1986)

Martin I. Lorin, *The Parents' Book of Physical Fitness for Children* (Atheneum, New York, 1978)

Ann Holdway, 'Eating Backwards', *In Touch*, Newsletter of the British Touch for Health Association, no. 18, February 1987

Maurice Hanssen, *The New E for Additives* (Thorsons, 1987)

Peter Mansfield and Jean Monro, *Chemical Children* (Century Hutchinson, 1987)

Susan Lewis, *Allergy? Think About Food* (Wisebuy, 1984)

Hyperactive Children's Support Group, The Secretary, 59 Meadowside, Angmering, West Sussex BN16 4BW

Stress and relaxation

It is now recognized that children not only need a reasonable amount of stress, in the form of mental and physical stimulation, but that they can also suffer from too much stress. Children may encounter many stressful situations or events in their daily lives, ranging from the loss of a parent by death or divorce to being ridiculed in class, performing in public or being late for school.

Children react to stress in many different ways. Too much stress may result in emotional and behavioural problems and it may spark off particular disorders, especially those for which a child already has an inherited disposition. Some of the physical reactions to stress include breathing difficulties, tummy upsets, skin eruptions, frequent minor illnesses and sleeping problems. Emotional and behavioural problems include aggressive behaviour, irritability, and learning difficulties. While children have their individual reactions to stress, it has also been found that boys tend to react differently to stress from girls, in that they respond more with aggression and difficulties with concentration, while girls tend to become more withdrawn and tearful.

Relaxation techniques

Although some stress is normal in a child's life and some reactions to stressful situations are quite common, it is now also considered possible and useful to teach children how to cope with stress and how to relax in an effective way. These days a lot of attention is being paid to stress and to healthy ways of dealing with it and more and more people are learning relaxation techniques. Many of these techniques can also be used for children.

Apart from having their children learn relaxation techniques, either at home, in school or in special classes, an important way parents can help their children to deal with stressful situations is by learning themselves how to relax and how to cope effectively with stress in their own lives. As with the consumption of food, children tend to copy their parents' stress-release patterns and if parents themselves succeed in finding healthy ways of releasing stress, their children may also be more inclined to do so.

One purpose of teaching relaxation techniques to children is to help them to become aware of the difference between feeling tense and relaxed. To tell a child or a group of children to relax makes little sense if they are not aware of the fact how tense or tight their bodies are. Many of the relaxation exercises that are suitable for children therefore begin by telling them to clench their fists or to stamp around. Then, when they are being told to relax, or, rather, to become all floppy, children will begin to notice the difference between the two states.

Relaxation exercises for children can be made into fun activities that can be part of physical education lessons at school or, indeed, can be introduced as a party game. As children grow older, the techniques become more sophisticated and can include work with a partner and testing each other's muscles for tenseness and relaxation.

One particular form of relaxation technique that is gaining popularity is autogenic training or autogenics — a therapy that proclaims itself as 'better meditation than medication'. It was first developed early in the twentieth century by a German neurologist called Johannes Schultz and one of his disciples, Wolfgang Luthe. The training, given in group-sessions or on an individual basis, should always take place under professional supervision. It consists of a series of gentle exercises in body awareness and physical relaxation that are easily learned. After having been taught the technique, the exercises should be practised at home several times a day, which makes autogenic training into a form of self-help.

Autogenic training is not very suitable for young children and, in fact, most people who learn autogenics are adults who want to prevent or are suffering from stress-related conditions such as high blood pressure, insomnia or migraine. However, it has been found that children from ten upwards can learn the technique and can benefit from it, especially in avoiding or lessening feelings of stress and anxiety.

Further information
Jane Madders, *Relax and Be Happy, Techniques for 5–18-year-olds* (Unwin, 1987)
Bonnie Remsberg and Antoinette Saunders, *Help Your Child Cope With Stress* (Piatkus, 1986)
Centre for Autogenic Training, 101 Harley Street, London W1N 1DF (tel: 01-935 1811)

Yoga

Yoga was introduced in the West in the nineteenth century, but it didn't begin to reach a wider audience until the 1970s. Now it is one of the most popular forms of alternative health care and yoga classes are being offered in many natural health centres and adult education institutes.

There are many forms or schools of yoga, although for untrained people it is sometimes difficult to recognize the differences between them. The form of yoga that is most commonly used in the West, and which is perhaps most adapted to Western ideas, is hatha yoga. It consists of a series of exercises, posture exercises as well as breathing exercises, which aim at creating a healthy mind in a healthy body. Although its therapeutic qualities are now also generally recognized, in particular for digestive problems, stress-related conditions and backache, yoga is most commonly regarded and used as a form of preventive health care.

Yoga has become an established and popular system of exercise for adults of all ages, but yoga for children is not, as yet, a very common thing. It would seem that children are too young to achieve the kind of mind–body control that yoga aims to develop and are not old enough to need the exercises as a means to release stress. Also, the discipline and concentration needed for the exercises don't seem particularly geared towards children and would even make it seem a little tedious to them. However, yoga for children is something that seems to be gaining ground. In Peter and Fiona Walker's book called *Natural Parenting*, yoga exercises form the basis of an exercise routine called 'jungle games'. Yoga postures that imitate the

movements and postures of animals, such as the ostrich and the cobra, are put into a sequence and linked by a jungle story. While listening to the story, the children are encouraged to imitate the animals they encounter and in this way they are practising some standard yoga postures in a playful manner. It is suggested that parents can do these exercises at home with their children and that children as young as two or three years old can participate in this kind of exercise.

If, for young children, the main purpose of yoga is to improve strength and flexibility and to retain their natural suppleness instead of later having to regain it by hard work, for school-age children the relation between body and mind already begins to feature and yoga exercises are thought to be useful for dissolving tension and as part of the experience of becoming more centered (see also page 50).

Another form of yoga that seems suitable for children is called Oki-do yoga, a form of yoga with both dynamic and relaxing aspects. It was developed in Japan by Masahiro Oki, who introduced it to the West in the 1970s. Oki-do yoga combines Indian yoga, Eastern healing methods and martial arts and, apart from traditional yoga exercises, includes work with a partner and group activities. For children, attention is being paid to exercises for acquiring a good posture as well as to dynamic and creative activities such as running and drama. Yearly summer camps are organized in Europe where children have their own Oki-do yoga programme running concurrently with a programme for adult participants.

Further information

Peter and Fiona Walker, *Natural Parenting* (Bloomsbury, 1987)

Gay Hendricks and Russel Wills, *The Centering Book* (Prentice Hall, Inc., New Jersey, 1975)

Gay Hendricks and Thomas B. Roberts, *The Second Centering Book* (Prentice Hall, New York, 1987)

Masahiro Oki, *Meditation Yoga* (Japan Publications Inc., Tokyo, 1979)

The International Centre for Active Birth, 55 Dartmouth Park Road, London NW5 1SL (tel: 01-267 3006) — organizes yoga classes for young children

British Wheel of Yoga, 80 Leckhampton Road, Cheltenham, Gloucestershire (tel: 0232 23889)

Yoga for Health Foundation, Ickwell Bury, Biggleswade, Bedfordshire SG18 9EF (tel: 0767 27271)

Oki-do Yoga, Basement Flat, 45 Elgin Crescent, London W11 2JD (tel: 01-727 1575)

Massage

Although the importance of touch for babies is now more generally recognized and most parents will cuddle and stroke their babies, while some will give them massage or will even let them sleep in the parents' bed, physical contact between parents and children often diminishes rather quickly as children grow older.

Nonetheless, growing children need touch too — both as givers and receivers. Children like to be held by their parents as a sign of love and reassurance, but they also like to touch in order to explore their surroundings — other people as well as animals and objects. On any infant or junior school playground, a lot of touching is going on, for example, holding hands or rough-and-tumble play. As children get older, however, the amount of touch between them may have reduced so much that it is practically non-existent — for boys more so than for girls, apart from some sports activities — until they start exploring touch in the context of sexual relationships.

One way to let children experience the benefits of touch is through massage, but, unlike babies, they need not only be receivers, they can also very easily learn to be givers of massage. Toddlers and young children, while clambering all over their parents in bed, may be shown how to give a parent a back rub, while older children

may be introduced to the idea of giving or receiving massage for instance, massaging each other's hands or feet when sitting watching television. Of course, giving or receiving massage should always be a completely voluntary activity — massage should never be experienced as intrusive in any way and both parties involved need to be in the right mood for it.

Self-massage

Adults and children who are unfamiliar with massage and feel shy about using their hands on other people may find it a good idea to begin with self-massage. Kneading, rubbing and stroking your own hands, legs or head, is an excellent way to explore various massage techniques and, apart from being a pleasurable and beneficial activity in itself, will give you an opportunity to find out what you like best, both as a giver and a receiver.

There are many different forms of massage. The one most commonly used in the West is called Swedish massage, developed in the nineteenth century by a Swede called Per Henrik Ling, but, in recent years, many traditional Eastern forms of massage have found their way to the West, such as shiatsu (see page 109) or taoist massage (see page 32), plus new massage techniques such as Rolfing (see page 107) have been developed in the West for specific therapeutic purposes.

When massage is required for a specific condition, it is best to go to a practitioner who is qualified to do a particular therapeutic form of massage. It is also perfectly possible and safe to learn some simple massage techniques for use at home as a form of preventive health care for parents and children alike, providing them with, as George Downing describes it in *The Massage Book,* 'a unique way of communicating without words'.

Further information
Jane Madders, *Relax and be Happy,* Techniques for 5–18 year olds (Unwin, 1987)
George Downing, *The Massage Book* (Penguin, 1974)

Reflexology

A particularly suitable type of massage for parents and children to practise on each other is massage of the hands and feet. It can be done while being fully clothed, except, of course, for socks and shoes, while doing something else in the meantime, such as watching television, although it is, of course, nice if both giver and receiver pay full attention to the massage going on, and it can be done in a short stretch of time.

A form of massage that focuses on the hands and feet and that is fast gaining popularity is called reflexology or zone therapy. It is based on the proposition that certain parts of the feet and hands correspond to certain parts and organs of the body. Massage and stimulation of specific zones on the feet will bring about better functioning of the specific organs they relate to and also encourages general relaxation.

The principles of reflexology have probably been known in Eastern countries for thousands of years, but it was only rediscovered in the West in the early twentieth century and began to reach a wider audience in the 1930s through the efforts of an American woman called Eunice Ingham.

A trained reflexologist or zone therapist will treat people for all sorts of conditions, especially those related to stress or any form of congestion. Used as a self-help technique, reflexology is considered particularly effective for relaxation and can thus function as a form of preventive health care.

Further information
Kevin and Barbara Kunz, *Hand and Foot Reflexology*, The unique self-health approach to wellness (Thorsons, 1984)
British Reflexology Association, 12 Pond Road, London SE3 9JL (tel: 01-852 6062)

Aromatherapy

It is argued that the only really good way to do massage is with oil and that vegetable oils such as olive oil, safflower oil, or almond oil are to be preferred to mineral oils. In addition to these vegetable oils, aromatherapy is sometimes used as a means to enhance the therapeutic effect of massage.

Aromatherapy is based on the use of essential oils or aromatic essences that are extracted or distilled from plants and trees, using the roots, leaves or resin. The origin of aromatherapy goes far back into history, but in recent decades there has been a renewed interest in the use of essential oils for medicinal purposes. The essential oils are known for their healing effects for particular physiological symptoms, while it is also believed that certain smells can have beneficial results for people who suffer from anxiety or depression.

Essential oils can be used by steam inhalation, in baths or footbaths and for massage. In the same way as certain smells may cause people to hold their breath or even may bring on an allergic reaction, other smells or aromas can be experienced as particularly beneficial, by encouraging deep breathing and inhalation and by relieving feelings of anxiety. When essential oils are being used for massage, they are good for the skin itself and, at the same time, can have a generally relaxing effect. In the case of a general relaxing massage, essential oils are mostly used in a diluted form by adding a few drops to a carrier oil such as almond oil. When used to massage a specific trouble spot, they can be applied neat.

In case of a particular disorder it is advisable to consult an aromatherapist who, after a discussion of the symptoms, will be able to select the appropriate essence, or a mixture of essences, and will advise you on the way it should be used. However, aromatherapy is also becoming increasingly popular for self-help, and many health shops now store a selection of those oils that are most commonly used.

Further information
Shirley Price, *Practical Aromatherapy*, How to use essential oils to restore vitality (Thorsons, 1987)
London School of Aromatherapy, PO Box 780, London NW6 5EQ
International Federation of Aroma-therapists, 46 Dalkeith Road, London SE21 8LS (tel: 01-670 5011)

Colour

Colour pervades our world, awake or dreaming. A world without colour would be almost unimaginable. However, colour is a phenomenon that far too many of us take for granted or just appreciate for its aesthetic qualities, while we remain unaware of the powerful effect it has on us.

Throughout the ages, many great civilizations have extolled and benefited from the use of colour as a powerful healing agent. Among these are the ancient Greeks in their colour healing temples, the Chinese, who utilized colour for diagnostic purposes, and the Tibetans, who used colour for mandalas (colourful spiritual pictures), chanting, and meditation.

Over the centuries this knowledge has been lost to the majority of people, except for a few dedicated individuals who have kept it alive and passed it on to others. In more recent times, Goethe is considered to have done very important research into colour, while Rudolf Steiner also included the importance of colour in his teachings (see also page 88).

Nowadays there is a renewed and growing interest in colour, in the influence it has on people and its therapeutic qualities. Each colour, from red to the blue and purple end of the spectrum, has its specific vibration that our body and mind can take in on various levels, which is illustrated by the fact that blind people can learn to tell which colour they sense under their hands.

Colour therapy

Colour therapy employs the healing power of colour frequencies for therapeutic purposes. One of the forms of colour therapy currently being practised uses machines that illuminate the body, or certain parts of the body, with certain colours. The colour frequencies are absorbed through the skin and will reach the various organs of the body via the lymphatic system. It is said that in this way colour can create, destroy or bring balance in the body's cells.

The application of the power of colour, however, need not take place only by means of colour therapy as used by trained colour therapists, for awareness of colour and its influences can be used in all our daily activities. Parents can be aware of the colours they use for their children, for their clothes, their meals and for their bedrooms. It is suggested that babies should not wear bright colours until the age of 14 months and that the traditional white baby clothes are indeed best — the assumption being that the very delicate and still vulnerable aura (energy field surrounding the body) of the child will be destroyed by colours which are too bright and the natural protection against outer influences will become weak.

A pastel colour from the blue range would suit a child who suffers from high fever, flu or general ill health. Bright red pyjamas would just enhance the very dynamic state in which the child is already and could make the child feel even more uncomfortable. Along similar lines, parents could use more blue colours for a hyperactive child's environment but red colours to stimulate the dynamic energy in children who are too quiet or withdrawn.

It can help children to enjoy their food more when it looks colourful — a joy for the eyes before being a joy to eat. One just has to look at the ice-creams and sweets that are on sale to realize that the commercial food producers and packagers are very well aware of the effect colourful food has on children, but, with a little effort, it is also possible to make healthy food look colourful and attractive by carefully combining naturally colourful foods together.

You may also want to consider the

colours of the walls in your house, especially the bedrooms. A bright red bedroom, say, would be likely to be a difficult place for a child to fall asleep in, but a neutral or pastel colour would be more relaxing.

Further information
Theo Gimbel, *Healing Through Colour* (The C.W. Daniel Company, 1980)

Theo Gimbel, *Form, Sound, Colour and Healing* (The C.W. Daniel Company, 1987), page 149
Living Colour, 33 Lancaster Grove, London NW3 4EX (tel: 01-794 1371)
Colour-Light-Art Research Ltd., Hygeia Studios, Brook House, Avening, Tedbury, Gloucestershire, GL8 8NS (tel: 045383 2150)

Psychic skills

It is sometimes argued that, apart from catering for their physical and emotional needs, parents should also encourage their children to listen to their 'inner voice' and to develop their psychic skills. It is also argued that doing so is an enjoyable and rewarding experience for all concerned.

It is believed that children may have mystical, spiritual or psychic experiences more often than we tend to think and that it is only because of parents' interference or disbelief that children begin to doubt their own experiences and consequently suppress them.

Whether or not one believes that children are more open to 'other dimensions' and have spontaneous spiritual or psychic experiences, it is true that they have fewer preconceptions about what is and isn't possible. Teaching children to see with their inner eye and to listen with their inner ear is easier than is sometimes thought and children often respond particularly well to exercises

designed to develop their psychic skills.

> *Before helping their children to develop psychic skills, parents are strongly advised first to gain some experience with these transpersonal exercises themselves so that they become familiar with higher or deeper levels of consciousness and learn to trust their own insights and intuitions.*

The first step in this process is learning how to feel centered or, as Gay Hendricks and Russel Wills write in *The Centering Book*, to 'experience one's psychological centre of gravity'. There is nothing mystical about feeling centered and the authors state that 'knowing how to feel centered is as important to young people as knowing how to read, write and brush teeth'. Further exercises to encourage the development of psychic skills include relaxation and breathing exercises, mental imagery or visualization, exploring dreams, focusing of energy, and healing.

Psychosynthesis

Psychosynthesis, a form of psychological therapy, was first developed at the beginning of the twentieth century by an Italian psychiatrist Roberto Assagioli. Psychosynthesis not only encourages people to fully develop each aspect — body, feeling life and mind — of their personality (personal psychosynthesis), but also advocates that people should go further than that and seek for transpersonal psychosynthesis, a process, as Diane Whitmore describes it in *Psychosynthesis in Education*, that 'enables the individual to explore those regions full of mystery and wonder beyond ordinary awareness, which we call superconscious — the wellspring of higher intuitions, inspirations, ethical imperatives and states of illumination'.

One way to learn some of these techniques is to take one of the courses in personal and transpersonal psychosynthesis, which are being given for both adults and youngsters on an individual basis or in groups, at centres for psychosynthesis that have been set up in many places in Great Britain, continental Europe and the USA.

Further information
Diane Mariechild, *Mother Wit* (The Crossing Press, New York, 1981)
Diane Whitmore, *Psychosynthesis in Education* (Turnstone, 1986)
Gay Hendricks and Russel Wills, *The Centering Book* (Prentice Hall, New Jersey, 1975)
Psychosynthesis and Education Trust, 3rd Floor, 188-194 Old Street, London EC1V 9BP (tel: 01-608 2231)

Hand healing

The tradition of psychic healing or hand healing goes far back into history and has often been associated with religious beliefs and practices. These days, however, with the growing interest in psychic phenomena, the use of psychic healing in a secular context is on the increase. Healing has a particularly strong following in Great Britain, where professional healers, in fact, constitute the largest group of alternative practitioners.

Hand healing is based on the assumption that psychic energy is generated by all living things and is

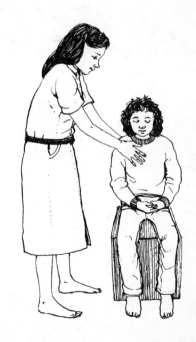

transferred between them. Psychic energy can carry emotions and other information and healing can be effected by focusing on this energy. Some people are more sensitive to these forms of energy and are better able to perceive and control it, and some of them will go on to become professional healers. A fairly recent addition to the many forms and uses of hand healing is called Therapeutic touch, which was developed in America in the 1970s by Dr Dolores Krieger. She advocates its use by nurses in hospitals and sees it as an adjunct to any other form of treatment a patient is receiving.

> *Psychic healing or hand healing is something that every person can learn and, in fact, many mothers use some forms of hand healing with their children often without realizing it. To lightly stroke a child who is feeling ill or to caress a knee that is hurt are forms of psychic healing everyone is familiar with, except that most people won't call it as such.*

There are simple exercises to learn to perceive and control psychic energy. Once people are familiar with psychic energy, they can develop their psychic skills to use them for healing purposes in the family and it is said that children may particularly like this kind of giving and receiving of energy. It is also argued by healers that psychic healing need not only take place when someone is ill, but that it can also function as a form of preventive health care, restoring a person's energy balance, making him more resistant to potential disease.

Further information
D. Scott Rogo, *Psychic Breakthroughs Today* (The Aquarian Press, 1987)
Dr Dolores Krieger, *The Therapeutic Touch*, How to use your hands to help or to heal (Prentice Hall, New Jersey, 1982)
Dr Michael Miller and Josephine M. Harper, *The Psychic Energy Workbook* (The Aquarian Press, 1986)
National Federation of Spiritual Healers, Old Manor Farm Studio, Church Street, Sunbury-on-Thames, Middlesex TW16 6RG (tel: 0932 783164)

PART TWO

Diagnosis and treatment

CHAPTER FOUR

The role of disease

The main difference between orthodox and alternative forms of medicine is perhaps not the way they treat illness when it occurs, but the way they look at why and when illness manifests itself in human beings. The differences in basic philosophy underlying the different approaches to medical care influence the way a diagnosis is made and, therefore, the way treatment is carried out. These differences of opinion concerning the role of disease apply to everybody — adult or children — but it seems that in some respects they are even more pronounced in relation to children.

Orthodox medicine

People who are the parents of today's children grew up in a time when medical science was making huge steps forwards in the fight against disease. New drugs and new vaccines were being discovered, new operation techniques were being explored (the first heart transplant took place in 1967) and generally there was a sense of optimism that doctors were beginning to have the upper hand in the battle against illness. This optimism is even more understandable when one realizes that the *parents* of today's parents grew up in a time when medical knowledge had not made as many advances and people, including children, still died of diseases that became curable or preventable by the time they themselves came to have children of their own.

The optimism of twenty or thirty years ago is still with us today. Medical science is still progressing at a fast rate, new discoveries are still being made and new life-saving techniques, especially when it comes to operating on people, are still being developed. Perhaps today's optimism is slightly more tempered than it used to be, partly because there is still no cure for cancer, while new diseases have emerged that need yet to be conquered (AIDS), and partly because the growth of alternative health care has started to bring into focus some of the shortcomings of orthodox medical health care.

The basic assumption underlying orthodox medical science is that the human body is like a machine, albeit a very complicated one. When someone falls ill, the cause of the illness is something that has come from outside (a germ or virus) disturbing the proper functioning of the machinery. By locating the site of the disturbance and removing the cause, the illness can be conquered and the person concerned will regain his or her health. In other words, all disturbances, causes as well as effects, are ultimately brought back to physical events and both diagnosis and treatment are based on these assumptions.

For the purpose of diagnosis, ever more sophisticated pieces of equipment are being used to pinpoint the exact character and location of the causes and disturbances. For the purpose of treatment many highly technological operating procedures have been developed that can often successfully restore the damage being done to a particular part of the body and drugs are being used that are increasingly specific in the fight against certain symptoms and diseases.

This is not to say that orthodox medical knowledge has always ignored the non-physical side of disease. With the development of Freud's psychoanalytical theories, it gradually became accepted that the mind can play a role in the manifestation of a disease of a certain person. The term psychosomatic illness was invented, but with it came a great deal

of confusion as to its use and validity.

Over the years the acceptance of the phenomenon of psychosomatic illness seems to have been fairly capricious. At times, the fact that the origin of certain physical symptoms was seen as 'all in the mind' meant that nothing much could be done about those symptoms. At other times, when new germs, viruses and allergies were being discovered as underlying specific conditions, the mental state of a patient was thought to be irrelevant and treatment would concentrate only on the physical causes and symptoms.

These days, orthodox medical knowledge has developed a somewhat more balanced view of the influence of the mind on physical processes and it is believed that someone's state of mind can have an influence on the course of a disease. However, psychological factors are not really seen as playing a role as a cause of illness, except perhaps in the case of stress, nor as an excuse not to treat the physical symptoms.

Even if today, at least partly spurred on by the growth and success of alternative medicine, the orthodox medical world is developing a somewhat more holistic outlook, where the interplay between body and mind is recognized to some extent, the major successes of orthodox medical science still lie in the realm of defining, locating and modifying purely physical events.

Children

Paediatrics, the branch of orthodox medicine concerned with illnesses of children, has successfully directed its efforts at fighting childhood illnesses and infant mortality. While only a few generations ago too many children died too young of childhood illnesses and other infectious diseases, these illnesses no longer pose a major threat to today's children in the Western world. It is even put forward that children no longer need to suffer from childhood illnesses at all, as successful preventative health care in the form of full-scale vaccination programmes could make these illnesses a thing of the past.

Also in the area of ante- and postnatal care, medical science has developed many new techniques aimed at saving the lives of new-born babies. The age at which a prematurely born baby has a chance of survival has been brought back dramatically and this is a notable achievement. Children now also undergo operations that weren't considered possible only a few years ago and, in short, the ability of the medical world to save lives has certainly had a dramatic impact on the scope of medical care for children.

When a child does fall ill from one of the many minor or not so minor illnesses that tend to be common during childhood, such as colds, flu and ear and throat infections, the development of painkillers and antibiotics has had an immense influence on the way children are being nursed at home. The orthodox medical view is that these days there is no need for children to suffer and that fevers and pains can and should be suppressed. Until recently junior aspirin, and nowadays children's paracetamol, have been advised as standard home medicines to relieve fever

and pain, while antibiotics are being prescribed for almost any infection that occurs.

> ## 'Children healthier 35 years ago'
> In spite of the great advances made by modern medicine, today's children are not healthier than the children of a few decades ago. According to findings by the Medical Research Council, the number of cases of eczema, asthma and juvenile diabetes have risen dramatically over the past 35 years and there have been substantial increases in hospital admissions of children up to the age of four.
>
> 'Children healthier 35 years ago', *The Guardian*, 10 September 1985.

As with orthodox medical care for adults, the improvements in medical care for children are predominantly in the area of drugs and technical know-how. Only recently, for instance, has orthodox medicine begun to recognize some of the psychological needs of new-born babies, while the phenomenon of psychosomatic illness in children is thought to be an even more difficult area to grasp. When physical disease is ruled out as underlying certain physical symptoms — for instance in the case of recurrent tummy aches — children are sometimes accused of 'pretending', while in the case of diagnosed physical illness, little attention is usually paid to psychological factors.

Preventive health care, other than by vaccination and immunization, hasn't played a significant role in orthodox forms of health care for children, although the recognition of the importance of sound nutrition for healthy children has quickly been gaining ground in recent years.

Further information
Adelle Davis, *Let's Have Healthy Children*, Updated by Marshall Mandell (Unwin, 1981)

Alternative medicine

To describe the philosophy underlying *all* forms of alternative medicine, lumping them all together, would seem to be almost preposterous, as there are so many different therapies that vary so much in their approaches to diagnosis and treatment. Yet, with respect to their basic philosophy on health and disease, alternative forms of medicine share a common outlook and it is this common view that distinguishes them, as a category, from orthodox or conventional medicine.

What all alternative therapies have in common is that they strongly emphasize the need for preventive health care. In orthodox medicine, preventive health care is mainly associated with vaccination programmes and periodical screening for cancer and other major diseases, but the sort of preventive health care advocated by alternative therapists has to do with lifestyle. Healthy food, sufficient exercise, effective ways of dealing with stress — all are part of a way of living that is aimed at promoting health and preventing illness.

In line with the importance that is attached to a healthy way of living, many alternative therapists see themselves as health educators. After having diagnosed and treated a patient for a certain condition, a practitioner will often see it as an important, if not *the* most important task, to advise this patient on how to lead a more healthy life and to avoid similar or other health problems in the future.

While orthodox medicine often seems rather preoccupied with the causes and effects of disease, alternative forms of medicine are more interested in what constitutes health. Health is not merely defined as the absence of disease, but as a positive state of well-being in which body and mind work together to achieve and maintain a balanced state of harmony and vitality.

However, the fact that in alternative medicine the emphasis is on health rather than on disease doesn't mean that the diagnosis and treatment of illness do not play an important role. However, rather than viewing disease as something that hits people at random and that has to be suppressed as radically as possible, most forms of alternative medicine regard illness as something that has a *meaning*, either for an individual or for a group of people or society. For it is an undisputed notion in alternative medicine that both mind and body play a role in health and disease. Although many therapies work mainly on the physical body and there are also therapies that mainly concentrate on psychological phenomena, *all* therapies recognize that there is a link between body and mind and use this link for diagnosis and treatment.

Some therapies, and indeed some therapists, will concern themselves more with the meaning of disease than others and some will attach more significance to psychological factors than others, but the common viewpoint is that an illness, when it occurs in a person, reflects an imbalance in that person which can and should be corrected. This is also linked with the way the cause of an illness is viewed: not as a random attack of disease-causing germs or viruses on a defenceless person, but as a successful inroad made by those omnipresent germs and viruses on a system whose defence system has been weakened by a temporary or continuous state of imbalance.

From this it follows that the nature of the *imbalance* rather than the nature of the *germs* and *viruses* is the issue that receives the most attention in alternative medicine — quite the opposite from orthodox medicine, where the germs and viruses themselves are the main focus of research and study.

Where therapies differ is in the ways they consider the causes of the imbalances, both the nature of the cause and importance attached to it, and the ways in which the imbalances are treated. Some therapies (for instance homoeopathy) delve into a person's physical and psychological past problems in an effort to find the root cause of a problem before treatment can be implemented; other therapies, for instance osteopathy, focus more on present

structural imbalances and treatment is aimed at correcting those. In all alternative forms of treatment, however, the patient is being informed of the nature of the imbalance and is invited or, rather, urged to make those adjustments in his or her lifestyle — for instance by adopting an improved diet, by working on better personal relationships, or by changing his or her posture — that will promote healing and avoid the same or other imbalances occurring. For if it is thought that an illness reflects a certain imbalance in a person and, as such, has a certain meaning for that individual, it is also assumed that you can *learn* from the meaning of your particular disease.

> In the same way that disease has meaning for an individual, it can also have meaning for a group of people, particularly for a family or, indeed, for society as a whole. For instance, the current prevalence of chronic conditions and of conditions that affect the immune system is regarded by many people working in alternative medicine as evidence of imbalances in society as a whole, particularly with respect to the food we eat and the frequent use of antibiotics and vaccinations.

Children

Unlike orthodox medicine, alternative medicine has no special branch that is devoted solely to the treatment of children. Rather, each therapy has developed, to a greater or lesser extent, its own ways of treating children's conditions (see also Chapter 6). Even so, if various therapies differ in the techniques or remedies they use, they share some common underlying principles with respect to children's health care.

In alternative medicine the importance of preventive health care for children is probably stressed even more than it is for adults. Therapists frequently mention that they would like to see a child as early in his or her life as possible — especially practitioners of a 'system of medicine', such as anthroposophical medicine, homoeopathy or herbalism. They feel that a child treated according to their principles and with their remedies from the very beginning will have a better chance to enjoy good health in adult life. It is considered even better if preventive health care for a child begins before the child is born, or even conceived, as children are given a better start in life if their parents are eating a balanced diet and adhering to a healthy lifestyle.

There are also therapies, for example cranial osteopathy and chiropractic, that do not so much provide on-going paediatric care, as aim at the early discovery and treatment of imbalances, in particular structural imbalances. Practitioners of these therapies say that the younger a child is checked and treated (cranial osteopaths get to see babies as young as a few hours old), the more likely it is that health problems can be prevented later on in life.

At the same time parents are reminded that even optimum preventive health care is no guarantee that a child will never become ill. It is actually argued that children 'need' to fall prey to certain illnesses and that it is better for them to go through these illnesses than it is to suppress them or try to prevent them altogether.

Childhood illnesses are considered to serve a *function* by enabling the body to discharge certain imbalances, whether these imbalances stem from the prenatal period, early babyhood or the ever-changing internal and external circumstances later on in a child's life. Seen in this light, illness is, in fact, considered as a sign of a child's natural strength, of its ability to adjust to growth and change. In other words, it is healthy for a child to be ill occasionally. Moreover, by going through the usual childhood illnesses, a child will build up his or her immune system and having had a childhood illness not only ensures immunity for the rest of someone's life, it can also prevent chronic disease in later years (see also page 35).

If the common childhood illnesses are thought to have a certain physical *function* in a growing child, alternative medicine also looks at the *meaning* of illness in childhood, particularly of conditions that either seem more accidental or are more chronic in nature. This is where the belief in the psychosomatic nature of childhood conditions comes into focus.

Without disregard for the physical symptoms, illness is often seen as an expression of the psychological needs of a child. These needs can reflect a stage in the child's own personal development or, as can also be the case, they can be a reflection of the relationships in a family for which the child feels or is given a certain responsibility. Asthma is often regarded as a typical example of a psychosomatic condition in that it would be the result of the child's own suppressed emotions or of unresolved conflicts in the family.

The belief in the psychosomatic nature of illness and in the important of the family setting is also illustrated by the fact that even a predisposition to a certain illness is not necessarily seen as a genetic phenomenon, but, according to John Harrison in *Love Your Disease*, as something that is passed on in families 'through the messages parents give their offspring and the living habits and diet they pass down'.

Instead of fearing illness in their children and seeing it as something that should be avoided as much as possible, parents are urged to consider it as a natural part of growing up. Moreover, it is often suggested that parents should be encouraged to learn from the meaning of illness when it occurs in their children, for the sake of their children's development as well as their own.

Further information

George Vithoulkas, *Homoeopathy*, Medicine of the new man (Thorsons, 1985)

Dr John Harrison, *Love your Disease*, It's keeping you healthy (Angus & Robertson, 1984)

Natural Childcare, the macrobiotic approach to raising a healthy family (East West Journal Publishing, Massachusetts, 1984)

Edwin H. Friedman, *Generation to Generation* (The Guildford Press, New York, 1985)

The importance of self-help

One of the fundamental premises of alternative health care is that people should feel responsible for their own health and many practitioners in alternative medicine see themselves as health educators as much as professional healers. For adult patients this frequently means that they are urged to become more aware of their own physical and emotional needs and to adopt a more healthy way of living.

In the case of children, it is, of course, the parents who are responsible for their children's health care, but, apart from stressing parents' responsibilities, alternative practitioners also encourage parents not to just follow up professional advice, but to have more trust in their *own* healing abilities.

In orthodox medicine, much of the medical care has become very complicated and technical, needing the skills of highly trained people. In alternative medicine, a great deal of the health care on offer relies on fairly simple techniques that are easy to learn. This is not to say that there are not also highly trained and skilled professionals in alternative health care using techniques that only they can apply, but even those therapists will often teach their patients some self-help techniques they can do at home.

One of the assumptions of alternative

medicine is that every person possesses an ability to heal and that parents in particular should learn to develop these abilities and use them with their children. Trust plays an important part in this process — trust in one's own abilities and trust in the self-healing power of the body. This trust should replace the fear that many parents instantly experience when anything is the matter with their child. It is argued that orthodox medicine, by urging parents to rely on the medical experts, has made them more anxious and less capable of dealing with even minor symptoms and complaints, as a result of which parents are sometimes even seen to use hospital emergency services for their children for such minor complaints as common colds and sore throats.

Alternative practitioners want to educate parents away from fear, fear being seen as the result of lack of information, and replace this with self-confidence and a trust in the self-healing mechanisms of the human body. The example typically given is the way fevers are being treated. The orthodox approach is to suppress fever, while alternative medicine regards fever as the body's natural way of reacting to and dealing with the illness. As described in *Natural Childcare*, The macrobiotic approach to raising a healthy family, parents are urged not to rely on paracetamol but are being motivated instead

'to ride out the fever and not overreact. If you can be responsive and attentive, this may be the best way to learn about your child's inner balances and allow

him or her to heal without outside interference … You may have to spend more time in dealing with your child than you would if you were treating him with medication, but the result will be worth the extra effort.'

It is true that the orthodox medical world is now also beginning to recognize the important role parents can play in their child's recovery. Children's hospital wards now allow parents to be around much more and even encourage them to stay, while not very long ago parents were considered as just standing in the way of proper medical care.

Developing one's healing abilities is usually not something parents can do overnight. It is a gradual learning process that may begin, for instance, when parents take up baby massage. Seeing one or more alternative practitioners over a certain length of time can also result in the parent learning various self-help techniques or nursing skills for use at home. There are also evening or weekend courses where people can learn all sorts of aspects of health care, ranging from nutrition to massage, from herbal and homoeopathic remedies to yoga and meditation. Such courses can give parents' confidence an enormous boost, enable them to deal with their own or their family's health problems and have the added benefit of giving them the opportunity to meet other parents who are trying to do the same thing.

> *Apart from the fact that a confident and positive attitude from the parent is reassuring to an ill child, it is also argued that when parents are seen by their children as having a trust in their own abilities and in the natural self-healing power of the child's body, the children themselves become more confident, not only to rely on their body's own natural power for health but also to trust their own healing abilities when they become parents themselves.*

Further information
Natural Childcare, The macrobiotic approach to raising a healthy family (East West Journal Publishing, Massachusetts, 1984)
Joseph Chilton Pearce, *Magical Child* (Bantam Books, New York, 1980)

CHAPTER FIVE

Using alternative therapies

Why parents opt for alternative therapies

The fast growth of complementary or alternative medicine in recent years is frequently seen as a condemnation of orthodox medical care, but when you talk to parents who use alternative health care for their children, you will find that they have many reasons for doing so and that these reasons need not always be based on dissatisfaction with the orthodox medical world. Indeed, most parents who use alternative therapies will use the services of orthodox medical care as well (see also page 79), but they feel that there are times when they need something more or they need something different to that which orthodox medicine can offer.

Parents who use alternative therapies for their children can be divided into two main groups: those who have used alternative or complementary medical care for themselves before using it for their children and those whose first encounter with other forms of medicine is with and because of their child.

Parents who use alternative forms of medicine for themselves are the most likely ones to also use this type of medical care for their offspring and in some families the use of an alternative therapy, for example homoeopathy, already goes back one generation or more. However, there are many people who are not particularly aware of issues related to health care or who question the medical care on offer, until they become parents themselves.

Being responsible for one's own health is one thing, but being responsible for another person's health is quite a different matter and, all of a sudden, parents find themselves faced with choices and decisions regarding their child's health. It sometimes seems as if medical matters dominate a young child's life and, indeed, childhood is one of the periods in a person's life when the health services are frequently used.

Pregnancy and childbirth

From the moment a woman finds that she

is pregnant the notion is impressed upon her that it is the *baby's* health she should take into account even more than her own and the orthodox medical world seems best equipped to monitor the growth of the foetus, ensure a safe birth and provide the necessary aftercare for the baby. Sometimes, though, it is precisely the experience of pregnancy and birth that can make parents, whether or not they had previously used other forms of medicine for themselves, more conservative or indeed more radical with regards to the future health care of their baby.

If, during pregnancy, labour and delivery, and after the baby was born, it seemed that orthodox medical care with all its technical know-how and facilities saved the baby during a difficult process, the parents will naturally be extremely grateful. They have every reason to be so, for it is obvious that orthodox medicine has the knowledge and means to save a life that otherwise could have been lost. Moreover, a baby with serious health problems from birth will obviously stay under close medical supervision and the parents will have little reason or scope to try out other forms of medical care.

However, it is also during and after birth that new parents may begin to feel that there has been too much medical and technical intervention in an otherwise natural process. They can feel that, although orthodox medicine has solved many technical problems, it has taken away some essential elements of the experience of birth (see also page 18). As a result of this new awareness, they may then come to the conclusion that they want to explore forms of medical care other than the orthodox one.

Vaccination

The next moment in time when parents are confronted with a choice between orthodox and alternative forms of medical care is when their child is due for vaccination. Whether or not to have your child vaccinated is a difficult decision for parents and it seems to be a choice that they have to make amidst opposing views from the orthodox and the alternative medical worlds.

Parents who have used alternative therapies for themselves, especially those who have been seeing a practitioner on a fairly regular basis, are in a good position to discuss these matters with this practitioner as well as with the GP or doctor in the baby clinic who is responsible for the vaccination pro-gramme. However, there now seems to be a growing number of parents for whom the questions or doubts they have with relation to their children's vaccination are the first instance when they begin to question orthodox forms of medicine. For these people, and indeed for all parents, it is of the utmost importance that they obtain as much information on the subject as possible. Apart from discussing matters with their GP, parents can also make an appointment with an alternative practitioner. However, alternative therapists always stress that, when asked, they are willing to give their views, but that it is the parents who should make the decision (see also page 35).

> *Choosing for or against vaccination does by no means imply a definite choice between orthodox or alternative forms of medicine. Whatever parents decide for their child with regard to vaccination, they are still completely free to choose any form of health care for their child at any time for any problem.*

Baby and child care

The increased interest in matters of health care that many people experience once they have become parents need not focus only on matters surrounding birth or a specific question such as vaccination. When looking after a baby or a young child, you are responsible all the time for the infant's emotional and physical well-being, in other words you are constantly concerned with matters of health care. Moreover, as a parent you are not only responsible for keeping your child healthy (preventative health care) but you also have to look after your child when it is ill. For many people, nursing a sick person occurs for the first time when they have become a parent.

In all these matters of baby and child care, parents turn to the medical world for advice and the orthodox medical world provides many answers. It has set up baby clinics; it has, as we have seen, developed a whole branch of medicines specializing in children's illnesses (paediatrics); it has instituted children's wards in general hospitals and even built specialized children's hospitals. All these facilities are being used extensively and no one will

doubt the orthodox medical world's excellence in treating acutely ill children.

Yet, on a more day-to-day basis, for all those less acute illnesses and problems, there can, at certain times, be a mismatch between what parents need for looking after their child and what the orthodox medical world has to offer and this is when parents may turn to alternative forms of health care.

First of all, when consulting a practitioner, parents want someone who listens with a sympathetic ear, who takes ample time for the consultation and, perhaps most important of all, who respects the parents' own views and knowledge. Although in theory any health professional in the orthodox *and* alternative medicine world can fulfil these requirements, parents who have opted for alternative forms of health care often say that they find their needs better met by practitioners of alternative therapies. A contributory factor to this situation may well be that, compared with practitioners in orthodox medicine, a large proportion of practitioners in alternative medicine are women. When a mother brings her child for consultation and treatment (in most cases it is the mother who comes with the child) she may well feel more at ease talking to another woman, especially if she knows that the practitioner has children of her own.

Also, while in the orthodox medical world the parents are considered to be responsible for their children's health, as soon as a child falls ill, parents are all too often urged to hand over this responsibility to the doctor: the only thing a mother is told to do is to give the child the prescribed medicines at the right times and in the right dosage and then wait for the child to respond to the doctor's cure.

In alternative forms of medicine, more attention is usually paid to the parents' role in actually nursing a sick child. Rather than urging parents to just rely on the 'experts' and on drugs, alternative practitioners tend to give a lot of practical advice on nursing care and they often encourage parents to be more confident and trust their own healing abilities (see also page 61).

Antibiotics

The sometimes over-abundant use of drugs, especially antibiotics, by orthodox practitioners is another reason why some parents begin to look for alternatives. When as a parent you have to put one strongly coloured concoction after another into your child, it is not surprising that you begin to wonder whether there is not a better way to promote health or, as one mother put it, 'the antibiotics were obviously good for the ear infections, but they were definitively bad for him'.

It is true that some alternative therapies also use medication, but the preparations used by, for instance, homoeopaths and medical herbalists are generally considered to be less invasive and aggressive than orthodox drugs. Also, in alternative medicine, remedies are hardly ever put forward as the only way possible to cure a disease, but rather are thought of as one of many possible means to restore a balance that has been disturbed by illness.

Chronic conditions and disabilities

There is one more reason why parents may turn to alternative forms of medicine, even if they have always used and trusted the orthodox medical care on offer in the past and have never before contemplated the use of the other forms of medicine, either for themselves or for their children. This is when parents are confronted with the fact that their child suffers from a chronic condition such as migraine or asthma or when they have a child with a mental or physical disability.

Chronic conditions are notoriously difficult to treat and usually the only answer orthodox medicine comes up with is the use of a lot of drugs that control the condition but do nothing to help the child overcome it. Alternative therapies do not offer miracle cures for such conditions, but parents often find that what they receive is more time and attention for the child's and their own specific needs. Also, they are offered treatment using a variety of methods and techniques that they feel help both them and the child cope better with the condition, even if it is not completely cured.

Parents who have a child with a disability often find themselves in a difficult position. The orthodox medical world provides a lot of care for children with disabilities, but yet parents may feel that they want to find out if there is something more or something different that they can do for their child. On the other hand, they may be very wary of trying yet another therapy, only to be disappointed yet again. It is often extremely difficult, both for practitioners and parents, to be completely realistic with respect to possible results of treatment for children with disabilities and there are only few practitioners of alternative therapies who have any experience in treating these children.

Parents need all the help they can get to care for their child and there are occasions where an alternative therapy can provide new insights or help that may prove beneficial for both the parents and the child. Also, it is noticeable that especially with respect to medical care for children with disabilities, some therapies that were first considered to be 'alternative' have proven themselves so effective and beneficial that they have become part of mainstream medical care, examples being the Bobath therapy (a special form of physiotherapy) for children with cerebral palsy and music therapy for children with mental disabilities.

Finally, parents of children with a disability may want to use alternative therapies for some of those aspects of their child's health care that are not directly related to the child's particular disability,

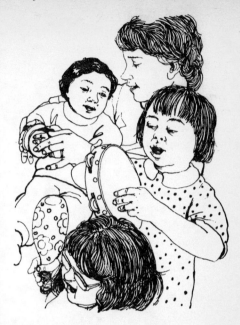

for instance homoeopathic or herbal remedies for colds or a light flu. Especially because they often have rather little choice with respect to the way their child is medically treated for his or her particular condition, some parents like to turn to alternative forms of health care for their child if and when they can.

Selecting a therapy

Once you have decided to use an alternative form of medicine for your child, how do you go about it? How do you know which therapy to choose from the sometimes bewildering array of therapies on offer?

One of the basic assumptions of alternative medicine is that it is holistic medicine, which means that its

practitioners say they treat the whole person — physically as well as emotionally — rather than dealing only with the symptoms. Most therapies, however, concern themselves with certain aspects of a person more than with others.

Broadly speaking, alternative therapies can be categorized into physical, psychological and paranormal or psychic therapies. The largest category is that of the physical therapies which in itself can be subdivided into therapies that work with remedies and diets, such as homoeopathy and naturopathy, and those that use some form of manipulation, such as acupuncture or osteopathy. A psychological therapy works on the mind only, for instance hypnotherapy, while an example of a paranormal therapy is hand healing.

Ways of choosing a therapy

When faced with the choice of which therapy to go for, there are basically three ways you can go about it:

● Decide which kind of method or approach you prefer for dealing with problems in general and health problems in particular — for example do you like a physical method, with an emphasis either on remedies and diets or on touch and exercise or do you like a more psycho-logical approach or perhaps a psychic one?

● Decide what kind of therapy would be most beneficial to your child's particular health problem.

● Find a therapist that you and your child can establish a good relationship with.

With respect to the first consideration, it is obvious that some people would feel far more at ease with one way of dealing with things than with another and this personal preference is very important in choosing a therapy, as it will influence one's relationship with the therapist. When you feel reasonably comfortable with the basic concepts of a particular approach, this will,

in all likelihood, result in a better working relationship with the practitioner, which, in its turn, will enhance the chances of successful treatment. Even so, it is important to remember that practitioners of physical therapies almost always concern themselves with the emotional and psychological aspects of their patients as well and that many therapists consider psychological counselling an integral part of their work.

With the second way, you would try to decide what kind of therapy would be most beneficial to your child's particular health problem. If a child seems to have an allergy problem for example, you may want to try a therapy that particularly deals with nutrition; if your child seems to have problems that are related to posture, a manipulative therapy would seem appropriate.

Although in theory this seems a sensible way to go about it, in practice it isn't always very easy. Although some therapies are sometimes considered particularly appropriate for certain health problems, it isn't really part of the holistic approach to single out particular forms of treatment for particular health problems. Also, a condition that seems, on the surface, to be the same for everybody, for instance, asthma, may still need a different approach for different sufferers, depending on whether the condition seems to have a more allergic basis, whether there are postural problems involved or whether psychological factors seem to play a more significant role.

The third consideration — a good rapport between the therapist and the patient — is the way in which many people choose a particular therapy, that is, they choose a therapist rather than a therapy.

The search for healing

Whatever way you select a therapy or find a therapist, it is important to remember that the first therapy or therapist you choose might not be the last one. Of course it is always possible that you 'strike it right' first time, that the relationship with the therapist is immediately very satisfactory — which means that not only the parent trusts the therapist, but that the child also likes him or her — and that the therapy seems to be effective, but it may also happen that the first therapy or therapist you opted for cannot offer you and your child all you need, something you may find out after one or after several visits. It is your prerogative to stop seeing that particular therapist and find another one who either uses the same therapy or a different one. 'Shopping around' for the right therapy and therapist is not only perfectly acceptable but also advisable because of the importance of a good working relationship between patient and practitioner.

Apart from the fact that *you* may want to try more than one therapy or therapist, it may also happen that a practitioner thinks your child needs more or a different type of treatment than he or she can offer and consequently will refer you to another therapist. Practitioners who work in a health centre and know their colleagues and the work their fellow practitioners are doing may sometimes be more inclined to refer their patients to someone else and,

if necessary, exchange information about a patient than practitioners who work completely on their own. Also, some children may benefit from treatment by several different practitioners at the same time, and the more various therapists know about each other's work and approach, the more chance there is that a child will receive an integrated form of treatment.

In the words of one alternative practitioner, this 'healing path' or 'search for healing' is

> 'as if there is a healing journey on which you have to go when you are ill and each person you come across is a step on the way. It's wonderful if I as a healer happen to be the final step in another person's journey, because then I think, "Ah, I got this person better." But it's not really true, it's just that he or she may already have gone a long way and I happened to be the one who provided the final help. Sometimes I may just contribute one special ingredient or one particular step in a person's journey and hopefully I gave something worthwhile on the way.'

One issue that may arise when you decide to go from one therapist to the next, is to how many different people are you going to take your child. If one therapist can't solve a particular problem, nor can the next one, when are you going to stop trying? There is no clear-cut answer to this question, but in the case of a child the answer is sometimes given by the child. Often he or she will get fed up with being dragged from one therapist to another before you do and alternative practitioners are usually not in the business of treating unwilling patients. However, in a good alternative practice, every consultation with a therapist may turn out to be a learning experience. There are occasions when the lesson to be learned is to stop trying for a while.

How to find a therapist

One of the reasons why it is sometimes more practical to choose the right therapist rather than to select a certain therapy is that, although many practitioners use only one therapy when treating patients, there are also a great many practitioners who employ more than one form of treatment: a naturopath may also use osteopathy, an acupuncturist may also use herbal medicines, a medical herbalist may also use psychological counselling, a chiropractor may also use applied kinesiology and almost all practitioners give nutritional advice. You will therefore find that it is often the practitioner who will decide which therapy to use rather than the person who comes for treatment.

To find the right therapist is therefore at least as important as finding the right therapy and, in the case of children, it can be argued that it is even more important. Treating children is not the same as treating adults and it is essential that you find a therapist for your child who has experience with children.

Word of mouth

The most common way people find an alternative practitioner is probably through word of mouth and there is a lot to be said for it. If someone *you* trust, trusts a particular therapist, then that is certainly a very good start in your search for a suitable therapist. There are, however, a few warnings to be given. First, the fact that your friend or relative trusts this practitioner shouldn't prevent you from finding out about his or her professional qualifications. Most national associations of alternative practitioners will allow only members with a certain degree of professional training on their register and, although membership of a national association of practitioners for that particular therapy is no absolute guarantee for professional conduct, it certainly helps (see also page 72).

Secondly, the fact that your friend or relative likes a particular therapist doesn't ensure that you too will like him or her. The personal rapport between practitioner and patient is very important and, if you feel that the therapist doesn't suit you as a person, you are under no obligation whatsoever to continue going there.

Last, but not least, if your friend or relative used this therapist for herself rather than for her child, you still must first find out whether the therapist has any experience in working with children before you decide to go and see her or him with your child.

Using your own therapist

This brings us to the next method of finding a therapist, which is common among parents who have used alternative forms of medicine for themselves before using it for their children. If you are such a parent, it would seem to make sense to ask a therapist who has treated you in the past, or is still treating you now, whether he or she can treat your child. Even more so than finding a therapist by recommendation, this ensures a relationship of trust between you and the therapist, although it doesn't necessarily guarantee that your child will also take to this particular person.

Once again, however, you should make sure that your therapist has been treating children before. A therapist who doesn't have experience with children should tell you so, and if he or she is not in a position to treat your child, he or she may know a colleague who is.

Referral by GP

A third possible way to find a suitable therapist is to get one recommended by your family doctor. There are doctors who are interested in alternative forms of health care and who personally know some alternative practitioners whom they trust and to whom they sometimes refer their patients if they feel the patients would benefit from this. Some doctors actually like to be able to suggest a different course of action for those conditions that are difficult to treat with orthodox medicine and, if the alternative practitioner is also trained in orthodox medicine, your GP may even supply you with a referral letter.

However, the number of doctors in the orthodox medical world who would follow this course of action is still very small and, by and large, relations between the two forms of medical care are rather more strained (see also page 79).

Professional organizations

A fourth and perhaps the most 'official' way of finding a therapist is by contacting one of the professional organizations that work in the field of alternative or complementary medicine. If you don't know a friend or relative who uses alternative therapies and if you dare not ask your doctor, getting the name of a qualified practitioner (preferably someone who lives or works near where you live or work) via a professional association is the safest way to proceed.

The professional organizations in the field of alternative medicine concern themselves with training standards and with working practices. To become a practitioner of a certain therapy, someone must usually have followed a three- or four-year full-time training course. If you obtain someone's name from an organization's list rather than from the telephone directory, you can be certain that this person is qualified as defined by the particular association and that he or she adheres to a professional code of practice, also as defined by that particular organization.

Unfortunately, the legal status of alternative or complementary medicine and their practitioners varies from country to country and from therapy to therapy. In some countries none of the therapies have statutory recognition, which means that anyone can call himself a therapist of some sort, while in other countries some but not all therapies are now legally recognized and protected. As long as this situation persists, it is up to the practitioners to organize themselves professionally as best as possible and it is up to the general public to be as discerning as possible when choosing a therapist and to always expect the highest standard of treatment. Together they must ensure that quackery — always a potential risk — cannot get a foothold.

When finding a practitioner via an official organization, you once again have to make sure that you get referred to someone who works with children. Practitioners are registered according to the therapy or therapies they use, but, so far, it hasn't been common practice to register if their particular interest is in working with children. However, if more parents would begin to ask this question it might be considered worthwhile to set up a separate register for 'children's therapists'.

Further information
Information Service, Institute for Complementary Medicine, 21 Portland Place, London W1N 3AF (tel: 01-636 9543) — will give you the names, addresses and telephone numbers of professional organizations and training centres for most alternative therapies. It can also supply the names of individual practitioners in acupuncture, chiropractic, homoeopathy, herbal medicine and osteopathy and can check the names of practitioners of these therapies and tell you whether they belong to one of the reputable professional organizations. Local volunteer Public Information Points hold this sort of information for their areas and can help you in the same way. The service publishes a yearly directory of UK practices, therapies and information.

Children's therapists

You will have realized by now that it is very important to find a therapist who has experience of working with children. The obvious next question to be asked is, which therapists are most likely to have that kind of experience?

To begin with, there are those practitioners who first qualified as orthodox medical doctors before learning the special skills involved in an alternative therapy. Typical examples are anthroposophical doctors and homoeopaths (although one doesn't have to be a medically qualified doctor to practise as a homoeopath). These people often work as family practitioners and, through their training and working experience are in a position to be familiar with children and children's illnesses.

There are other therapists who, by the nature of the therapy they use and the kind of conditions they commonly treat, also tend to function as 'family practitioners'. Examples are naturopaths and medical herbalists who, in the course of years of practice, are sometimes seen to have built up a group of patients where whole-family health care plays an increasingly important role.

The amount of attention that is paid during training courses to children and children's problems varies considerably from therapy to therapy, but, although some attention is usually paid to paediatrics, it is generally not considered to be one of the major topics. For many practitioners, the moment they begin to be interested in treating children doesn't arrive until they have become parents themselves. Until then, they may not have come across any children or children's problems, but becoming a parent can bring this area into focus. Therapists who become interested in treating children when they had previously only treated adults sometimes find they need some extra information or schooling.

The fact that, up to a certain moment, a therapy hasn't been commonly used for children, doesn't necessarily mean that this therapy isn't suitable for children. A case in point is acupuncture. It was introduced to the West for treatment of adults, but in China has always been used for children as well. Acupuncture is now also being used in the West for treating children and courses are now being developed to provide the relevant information on childhood conditions and their treatment by acupuncture.

There are also therapies that are particularly suitable for and used with children, such as cranial osteopathy. Any therapist who uses this technique will have experience in treating children, for, although it wasn't specifically developed for children, its subtle character and gentle approach makes it particularly appropriate for use with even very small babies.

Another group of professional healers who have experience with children are those who started training to become skilled in a particular therapy *after* they had become parents themselves. Whether or not they were already interested in or using alternative therapies before having children, some people become particularly interested in alternative health care for children because of their own experience as a parent. If such a person then decides to pursue this interest in a professional way, he or she is often particularly well placed to work with children.

Unlike in orthodox medical practice, where there are specialist doctors who treat only children, there are no such specialists in alternative medicine. As a matter of fact, the percentage of children seen by practitioners who are interested in and regularly work with children is often still only between five and ten per cent. Some notable exceptions are, for instance, cranial osteopaths and some (but not all) homoeopaths, up to a third of whose patients may be children. However, as more parents come for treatment for their children and as more therapists become parents themselves or parents become therapists, the number of practitioners who have experience in working with children will undoubtedly grow.

Already, in line with demand, some practitioners or groups of practitioners have begun to set up special children's clinics at certain hours during the week. For several reasons, this seems a particularly good idea. First of all, if a practitioner is running a children's clinic, it is obvious that he or she is interested in and has experience with children. Secondly, the hours can be set to accommodate working parents or parents with school-age children and Saturday mornings, for instance, seem to suit both groups. Also, if they run a children's clinic, practitioners often charge reduced rates or even treat children free of charge, and last but not least, it gives the parents who bring the children a chance to meet other parents and they can find out that they are not the only ones who have a particular problem or follow a particular course of action.

Consultation and treatment

The many different alternative therapies that exist all make use of different techniques and, in the next chapter, a number of therapies are described with reference to how they can be used for children. Apart from using a wide variety of methods and techniques, alternative practitioners also have individual styles and they may vary the approach they use with individual patients. Even so, and although details will vary, it is possible to give a general description of what to expect when visiting an alternative practitioner for consultation and treatment.

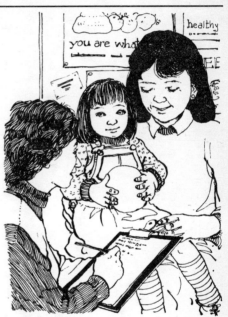

The first visit

When you make an appointment to visit an alternative practitioner for the first time, you will usually have to allow one or two weeks before the therapist can see you. These days, alternative practitioners are very busy people, and as it is common practice to allow ample time for each appointment — between 30 and 60 minutes — waiting periods to get an appointment have increased.

Tell the therapist, or receptionist in a group practice, that you will come with your child and that it is your first visit. Often, more time is allocated for the first appointment to allow time for taking a case

history. During your first visit, the therapist will usually take a case history and will explain what the actual treatment will involve. In order to get to know you and your child, the therapist will no doubt ask a lot of questions, but you should also feel free to ask as many questions as you like, especially with regard to the therapy in general and the specific treatment to be given. Questions you may want to ask are:

● What exactly does treatment involve?

● How many times are we expected to come back?

● Does treatment take place only at the practice or are we expected to do something at home as well?

● When can we expect to see any results?

As the consultation and treatment concern your child, always make sure that he or she gets involved in the discussion. Older children can give details about their condition themselves and they should also be encouraged to ask questions.

It may sometimes be a good idea if treatment is first demonstrated on the parent, especially in the case of treatment that involves manipulation. This can alleviate any worries about whether the treatment hurts, both for the parent and the child, especially if the parent is also unfamiliar with the therapy.

When there is still enough time, some treatment may take place during the first visit, but it is not unusual for treatment to be deferred until the second visit.

Payment

Before making your first appointment, or when you are making it, ask about fees and the usual way to pay them. By making these enquiries beforehand, you save yourself from being confronted with an unexpected sum to be paid at an unexpected moment. You will often find that the first visit, because it is longer, is more expensive than the following ones

and that you are asked to pay immediately after treatment rather than being sent a bill.

In most countries, alternative or complementary medicine by and large falls under private medicine, which means that comprehensive treatment by an alternative practitioner can become a rather expensive affair. There are some private health insurance schemes that pay for some forms of treatment but, although this can be considered as a step in the right direction, for many people it doesn't solve the problem of how to afford treatment. In England there are some doctors who practise in the National Health Service, which is possible if they are orthodox doctors who have then also trained to become a homoeopath or acupuncturist, but these practitioners are few and far between.

If you have difficulty paying for treatment, this need not mean that alternative health care is not for you or your child. Although some forms of treatment require highly specialized skills, there are also many forms of self-help available, and it usually isn't too difficult to learn some of these self-help techniques yourself. Also, there are some therapists, as we have seen, who charge lower rates for children or even treat them free of charge (see page 75). Also, teaching colleges of alternative or complementary therapies sometimes operate clinics, where you will be treated by students under supervision. The rates such clinics charge are usually lower than those charged by someone who runs a private practice.

Last but not least, mothers have been known to find their own creative solutions to payment problems by arranging to pay in kind rather than in cash, for instance, babysitting, cooking meals, shopping or, if you have some specialist skills yourself, giving music lessons or making clothes, are all ways in which people can pay others who need these services as much as they need money.

Seeing the child alone

Once treatment has started and a good relationship has been established between the therapist, the parent *and* the child, the therapist may sometimes suggest seeing the child without the parent being present. Of course, this applies only to somewhat older children and should happen only if all parties concerned feel absolutely comfortable about it.

The question as to whether children should have treatment on their own, without a parent being present, depends a great deal on how one sees the role of parents in their children's health care. If one believes that parents not only have the prime responsibility for their children's health, but are also very capable of judging their child's condition and looking after their child when he or she isn't feeling well, then it is obvious that parents should be involved as much as possible in every stage of treatment. As a consequence, parents would always be present during treatment and the therapist might even teach them some skills to encourage the healing process to be continued at home. Involving the patient in his or her own health care is, after all, one of the hallmarks of alternative medicine and, in the case of children, the parents would be the obvious people to involve as much as possible.

Occasionally, a therapist may feel that a parent, just because he or she is so closely involved with a child, would tend to get in the way of effective treatment and the situation would be improved if the parent was not in the room with the child. However, rather than asking a parent to leave the room, it could well be more effective to try and change the relationship between parent and child with everybody being present because this relationship will also influence the effects of treatment in the long run.

On the other hand, after a certain age, children should not only become more independent of their parents but also be made aware of the fact that they themselves can and should take responsibility for their own health care. If it seems, at a certain point during treatment, that a child would benefit from a diminishing amount of interference from the parent, it would seem to make sense for the therapist to see the child for treatment without the parent being present.

Whether or not, as a parent, you are present during every treatment session, the therapist should always inform you about the actual treatment being given and about any progress that is being made.

The healing process

It is not always easy to assess a healing process. If you have always been using orthodox forms of medicine you probably have got used to the 'instant cures' produced by orthodox drugs such as antibiotics. No doubt, orthodox drugs very frequently have an immediate and life-saving effect in emergency cases and, in more chronic conditions, orthodox medicine often alleviates the symptoms, sometimes also instantly, even if it doesn't always provide a more permanent cure.

In alternative forms of medicine, however, the healing process is not so much directed at alleviating symptoms as at restoring balance and calling upon the 'vital force' of the body as a whole to promote healing. Thus, when you try to assess an alternative treatment, you should not only look at what happens at a single treatment session, but more at signs of change *between* sessions.

Alternative forms of medicine don't provide wonder cures for your child, but it is also the case that alternative therapists who have worked with children have found that in many instances children have responded particularly well to their treatment. They have observed that especially those therapies and remedies that work in very subtle ways have, in fact, a greater chance of 'getting through' to a child's bodily system than to an adult's. It is thought that in a child the 'vital force' is particularly strong and that, because a child is still growing, his or her body is, by definition, geared towards change.

All this is not to say that disappointments or set-backs do not occur when your child is being treated with alternative medicine. Some conditions are more difficult to treat than others and some children are more open to treatment than others. When reading books on alternative therapies, you will find that they often typically describe only those case histories that have a successful outcome and your child's recovery after treatment by an alternative practitioner might well be less spectacular than you may have come to expect after having read about other people's case histories. On the other hand, it is also true that alternative practitioners get the bulk of their new patients through re-commendation by their former or current patients, which must imply that many people are well satisfied with the treatment they have received.

Treatment with any alternative therapy is generally considered to be free from undesirable side-effects. However, one thing to remember about the healing process is that, once treatment has started, there is the possibility that symptoms may temporarily get worse before they start getting better. This worsening of symptoms, or 'healing crisis', is part of the process referred to as the 'Law of Cure', which says that an illness often disappears in the reverse order in which it manifested iself. The 'Law of Cure' is particularly true in cases of chronic disease and it is the duty of practitioners to warn their patients about a possible temporary worsening of symp-toms and to help them to cope with them.

There should also be a word of warning. If your child has been receiving orthodox treatment in the form of drugs for a particular condition, you need to discuss this treatment with the therapist. Particularly in the case of chronic conditions, you should never stop the orthodox medication suddenly and you should be suspicious of an alternative practitioner who wants to throw out all orthodox drugs straight away. If the object of alternative treatment is to become less dependent on drugs, it can be achieved only by successful treatment, which, more often than not, will be a gradual rather than a speedy process.

Moreover, at any time during treatment, parents always have the right to ask as many questions about what is going on as they wish and they have the right to stop seeing a particular practitioner if they no longer feel comfortable or satisfied with the treatment their child is receiving.

The relationship between orthodox and alternative forms of medicine

Parents who consult alternative practitioners for their childcare can roughly be divided into two groups: those who use alternative forms of medicine for first-line treatment and orthodox medicine as a last resort, and those who primarily rely on orthodox forms of treatment, but who turn to an alternative practitioner when they feel that orthodox medicine is not helping them sufficiently.

It is obvious that this is only a rough division, for within these two groups many variations are possible. It is also clear, though, that all these parents, whether they belong to the first or to the second group, use both alternative *and* orthodox forms of medicine and that it is up to the parents themselves to decide what form of health care best meets their needs.

Parents who have relied on alternative forms of health care for themselves and their children for some period of time, usually have developed their own particular balance between the use of various forms of health care, although finding this balance is often a gradual rather than a quick process. However, if using alternative medicine is a recent choice, there are a few guidelines to be observed that will help you to use the services of both orthodox and alternative forms of health care in a way that best suits your own particular needs.

Diagnosis

When visiting an alternative practitioner for the first time, you should always first have checked the condition of your child with your family doctor, except if you are seeing practitioners who have also qualified in orthodox medicine, such as anthroposophical doctors and some homoeopaths, who are therefore in a position to give a diagnosis in the same way that a purely orthodox medical practitioner would. Any respectable and trustworthy alternative therapist should always ask you whether your child has been seen and diagnosed by a doctor.

The diagnosis as related by the parent — very occasionally supplemented by information from another alternative or orthodox practitioner (see also pages 70 and 72) — is taken as a starting point for the therapist to do his or her own investigations. By taking a case history and by using specific diagnostic techniques, which may vary from therapy to therapy, the practitioner will arrive at his or her own conclusions on which treatment can then be based. The conclusions arrived at by the alternative practitioner will sometimes confirm the diagnosis given by an orthodox practitioner, but it will also happen that it differs. Especially in the case of a general malaise or non-specific complaint where an orthodox diagnosis has detected no physical abnormalities, alternative practitioners are sometimes in a position to detect imbalances in a patient's body that orthodox medicine tends to overlook or ignore.

Some parents who have been using alternative therapies for their children on a regular basis always follow this course: they use their family doctors for an initial diagnosis and, except for treatment in real emergencies such as accidents or life-threatening conditions such as meningitis, they will turn to alternative forms of medicine for treatment.

As a lot of treatment by alternative therapies takes place through self-help, it cannot be stressed enough how important it is for parents to obtain a correct diagnosis, for although parents can quickly spot whether something is wrong with their child, they are not in the right position to make a proper diagnosis. One research showed that 73 per cent of mothers who consulted a GP had either not reached a diagnosis before the consultation or had made a diagnosis that was different from

the one made by the doctor. Seventeen per cent of mothers were told by their GP that their child's condition was more serious than they had thought.

Informing your GP

If parents should always inform the alternative practitioner of their dealings with orthodox medical care, should they also inform their family doctor — or a consultant whom they have been seeing for their child's condition — about their intention to visit an alternative therapist? In principle, yes, in practice, however, many parents feel that by telling an unsympathetic doctor thay they are using alternative therapies for their children, they may jeopardize their position with this particular doctor whom they may still need for future treatment or for emergency situations. For the reality is that many doctors within the orthodox medical profession do not particularly approve of alternative forms of medicine or even feel outright hostility towards them, although it is possible to detect a small but growing number among them who are becoming more interested in what other forms of medicine have to offer. Unless you know that a particular doctor has an open mind about these matters, you are likely to feel rather hesitant about informing your doctor about the fact that you are using any form of alternative treatment.

An ideal world

The orthodox medical world, on the whole, still seems to be rather suspicious of alternative medicine and tends to feel threatened by the growth of alternative health care and its popularity with the general public. However, in spite of the fact that increasing numbers of people are becoming interested in alternative health care, practitioners of complementary or alternative medicine still often feel under threat from the powerful medical establishment.

Although this situation is regrettable, it will not really change until the parties concerned, practitioners as well as patients, all decide to do something about it. In an ideal world, orthodox and alternative practitioners will work together, recognizing each other's abilities, each practising in those areas in which they are most capable without feeling threatened by one another.

Parents are in a prime position to see and value the merits of both orthodox and alternative forms of medicine, for if they use alternative health care for their children, they will still also use and rely on orthodox forms of health care. When the *consumers* of health care begin to see the different systems of medicine as complementary to each other rather than an either/or decision, *providers* of health care may begin to do the same. These days, when the term complementary medicine is being used, it always means to denote other forms of medicine being complementary to orthodox medicine. Maybe one day the time will come when we will begin to think of the various forms of medicine as being complementary to each other.

Further information
Berry Mayall, *Keeping Children Healthy*, The role of mothers and professionals (Allen & Unwin, 1986)
Roger Newman Turner, *Naturopathic Medicine*, Treating the whole person (Thorsons, 1984)

CHAPTER SIX
Alternative therapies for children

The list of all alternative therapies would be a long one (*The Alternative Health Guide* by Brian Inglis and Ruth West describes around 60 different therapies) and it is growing every year, with new therapies and variations on existing ones being added. In this chapter, therefore, I shall limit myself to describing, firstly, some of the more established therapies and, secondly, those forms of treatment that are particularly suitable for children. In all I have selected 14 different therapies and a few other therapies have been briefly mentioned or described elsewhere in the book, for instance autogenics, colour therapy and hand healing (see pages 42, 48 and 51).

The purpose of the descriptions is to help you on your way in deciding whether you want to find out more about a particular form of treatment. There are many books on the market that cover either one therapy or give an overview of a whole range of therapies and anyone who wants more detailed information on any therapy should be able to find this without too much difficulty. However, most of these books give very little or no information on how a therapy can be applied to children and this is where I have tried to make up for this shortfall.

If you send for information to any of the professional organizations listed in the following sections, please always enclose a stamped, self-addressed envelope.

Further information
Stephen Fulder, *The Handbook of Complementary Medicine* (Hodder & Stoughton, 1984)
Brian Inglis and Ruth West, *Alternative Health Guide* (Michael Joseph, 1983)
Dr Andrew Stanway (Ed.), *The Natural Family Doctor* (Century Hutchinson, 1987)

Acupuncture

Acupuncture has been practised in China for thousands of years. In the West, however, it is one of the more recently available therapies in the field of alternative medicine when compared with homoeopathy or osteopathy.

Ever since it was introduced to the general public in Europe in the 1960s, acupuncture has attracted a lot of attention and most people now know that acupuncture involves 'sticking needles into the body'. A lot of publicity was given initially to the spectacular use of acupuncture for pain relief and to the fact that in China it was even used to anaesthetize patients during surgical operations. It is less well known that the main use of acupuncture is as a therapy for particular diseases and it is important to realize that this is its main application in the West.

Acupuncture is based on the belief that a life-force or energy, called *chi*, flows in our bodies along pathways, or meridians, that correspond to the various organs. When the balance between positive and negative forces, or yin and yang, is disturbed, the body's energy flow also becomes affected and the person becomes ill. The object of treatment by acupuncture is to restore the balance between yin and yang.

In acupuncture a diagnosis is made by checking the twelve pulses — six in each wrist — that correspond to the main meridians in the body. During treatment, needles are inserted at certain points in the body and they are then either left in place for a while or gently rotated for extra stimulation. There should be very little or no pain involved. A typical session may last between 20 minutes and an hour, although for children a session is made shorter rather than longer. How many sessions are needed will vary from case to case, as does the rate of progress.

Acupuncture can be used as the sole therapy for a specific disorder, but it is also often used in conjunction with other forms of treatment, such as herbal remedies.

Acupuncture and children

Acupuncture is often considered in the West to be unsuitable for children. In China, however, acupuncture has always been used to treat children and one piece of evidence for this can be found in *A Barefoot Doctor's Manual*, a practical guide for China's paramedical workers that combines modern Western medical practice and traditional Chinese methods of diagnosis and healing. The Western medicine described includes the use of drugs such as penicillin and sulphonamides, but the main emphasis is on traditional Chinese medical care especially massage, acupuncture and herbal medicine.

The section on 'common infectious diseases' such as measles and chicken-pox includes treatment by acupuncture and so does the section on 'common paediatric ailments', which describes conditions such

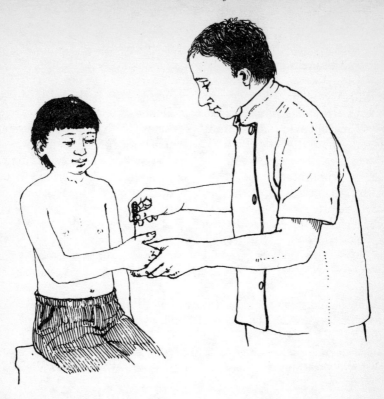

as convulsions, infantile diarrhoea and ear, nose and throat infections.

Recently some practitioners in the West have started to use acupuncture for children, in principle using the same technique with needles as for adults. Apart from straightforward acupuncture, a few other techniques are sometimes used, such as tapping a point instead of inserting a needle into it, or acupressure, during which the therapist uses his or her fingers to apply pressure at various points.

Acupuncture can be used for a wide range of disorders. Illnesses that have been treated effectively in children are: coughs, including bronchitis, influenza, glandular disturbances, constipation, diarrhoea, insomnia, teething, asthma, eczema, measles, whooping cough, urinary tract infections, nappy rash and the side-effects of immunization.

It is understandable that parents are sometimes apprehensive about taking their child for treatment by acupuncture and it is not usually thought of as a first line of treatment. However, an experienced practitioner should be able to allay the fears of both parents and child and it is often found that children respond remarkably well to this form of treatment.

The safety of acupuncture treatment

Recently, some people have become worried about the use of needles and the spread of AIDS. However, the Council for Acupuncture Fact Sheet of 11 February, 1987, states that the Communicable Diseases Surveillance Centre has confirmed that the sterilization procedures used by members of the Council for Acupuncture are effective against the AIDS virus. The code of practice for all membership associations of the Council covers the whole area of hygiene and safety for patients. This includes the health of the acupuncturist as well. The Council represents the British Acupuncture Association, the International Register of Oriental Medicine, UK, the Register of Traditional Chinese Medicine, and the Traditional Acupuncture Society.

Moreover, guidelines to ensure safe clinical practice issued by the Academy of Chinese Acupuncture to its members, include the use of single-use, pre-sterilized disposable needles. Finally, if patients wish to do so, they can buy their own needles and bring them to the acupuncturist to use for their own treatment.

Complementary Medicine, Journal of the Institute for Complementary Medicine, Newsletter (Supplement), January, 1987
Complementary Medicine Journal of the Institute for Complementary Medicine, Newsletter (Supplement), April, 1987

Further information
A Barefoot Doctor's Manual, Practical Chinese medicine and health (Gramercy, New York, 1985)
Julian Scott, *The Treatment of Children by Acupuncture* (Chinese Medicine Publications, 1986)

British Acupuncture Association, 34 Alderney Street, London SW1V 4EU (tel: 01-834 1012)
Traditional Acupuncture Society, 11 Grange Park, Stratford-on-Avon, Warwickshire CV37 6XH (tel: 0789 298798)

The Alexander technique

The Alexander technique was developed by F. Matthias Alexander, who was born on the island of Tasmania off the coast of Australia in 1869. In his early twenties he started a career as reciter, but during his performances he began to experience difficulties with his voice. He decided to try and solve his problems by himself, and, by analysing his posture and the way he moved, he subsequently succeeded in improving his voice.

In the course of the investigations into his problems with his voice, Alexander discovered many underlying principles about postural habits and how they influence someone's physical and psychological well-being. From this he developed his technique and, while still working successfully as a reciter — who was especially well known for his voice — he started teaching actors and members of his audience. In 1904 he moved to London, where he soon had a regular list of pupils. Since then, and after his death in 1955, Alexander's work has been continued all over the world.

The Alexander technique is thought of by its practitioners as an educational technique rather than a therapy. During a course of lessons, Alexander teachers encourage their pupils (who are never called patients) to change postural habits by helping them to increase their bodily awareness. While using his or her hands, a teacher will gently coach the pupil's body into adopting changes in posture and movement. Alexander teachers do not usually direct themselves to a specific problem or disease, but to the individual they are working with and it is often seen that an overall improvement of someone's bodily functioning will alleviate the *specific* physical symptoms. The Alexander technique is also widely taught to and used by actors and musicians to help them prevent or solve problems related to performing.

The Alexander technique and children

Healthy young children seem to have an inborn instinct for a natural and easy way of holding themselves upright, with a freely balanced head and lengthened spine. However, children can develop bad postural habits from quite an early age.

When we look at a child's physical development, it is possible to distinguish four causes of misuse:

● *forcing the child's physical development*

If children are made to sit up before their nervous systems have adequately matured, they loll about. This will result in the beginnings of misuse — their backs develop a sideways curvature. If children are left to adopt the sitting up position when they feel ready to do so, they will adopt a position where the back is balanced and upright and the head is in the position of Alexander's primary control — the proper use of the head and neck.

● *copying the bad example of parents*

Alexander teachers believe that many children's postural habits, good or bad, are due to copying their parents. As most parents, unfortunately, don't have good posture, many children end up with similar patterns of tensed shoulders and stiff movements.

● *fear*

It is thought that many bad postural habits are due to fear. Children have many fears, one of them being a fear of not being able to do things properly or not being able to do them at all. Fear causes tension in the body, resulting in its misuse.

● *school*

At school, with its emphasis on academic skills carried out sitting on chairs and at desks that are, by and large, the wrong shape and height, many bad postural habits have a chance to develop.

If misuse of a child's body can start early, it is also found that the Alexander technique can be beneficial in teaching children how to avoid it developing in the first place and that children from the ages of six or seven upwards can respond very quickly and successfully to the instructions of an Alexander teacher.

The Alexander technique can be taught to a child on an individual basis, but it is also possible to work with a group of children. Alexander himself was very interested in children and education and under his direction a school was opened in 1924 by Irene Tasker where Alexander's principles were applied to daily activities. Since then a few more attempts have been made to apply the Alexander technique in the school setting. One example of this is the work done by Jack Fenton, who in the 1970s carried out a programme in a number of English state schools.

Most Alexander teachers, however, work mainly with adults — one reason for this being that parents (and school teachers) are often not aware of the importance of good posture for children's physical and psychological well-being. There are also Alexander teachers who, although not specifically teaching the Alexander technique, use their skills and awareness in other teaching activities with children, in particular in teaching music or dance and movement.

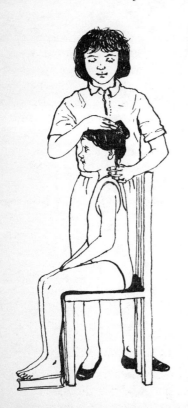

Apart from playing an important role in preventive health care, the Alexander technique can also help children to overcome particular problems such as difficulties with balance and coordination, tenseness, stuttering and difficulties with reading and writing. Moreover, the Alexander technique can also be beneficial for children with breathing problems, such as asthma, by helping them to improve their posture in general and their breathing in particular.

Further information
Wilfred Barlow, *The Alexander Principle* (Century Hutchinson, 1975)
Michael Gelb, *Body Learning*, An introduction to the Alexander technique (Aurum Press, 1981)
Society of Teachers of the Alexander Technique, 10 London House, 266 Fulham Road, London SW10 9EL (tel: 01-351 0828)

Anthroposophical medicine

Anthroposophical medicine is based on the teachings of the Austrian thinker and scientist Rudolf Steiner (1861-1925). Anthroposophy, the word being derived from the Greek words *anthropos* and *sophia*, meaning 'men' and 'wisdom', is a philosophy of life with a basis in Christianity. The basic principle underlying anthroposophical thinking is that human beings are seen as consisting of four components: the physical body, the etheric (formative) body or life forces, the astral (emotional) body or soul forces and the ego or spiritual forces.

Already during his lifetime Steiner's teachings gradually began to encompass most aspects of life as his followers applied his ideas to their own disciplines, be it education, agriculture, economics or, indeed, medicine.

Anthroposophical medicine is related to homoeopathy insofar as many of the medicines used are prepared according to similar principles (potentization) and are prescribed taking into account the whole person rather than just the symptoms of a particular disease (see also page 99). However, unlike homoeopathic remedies, which almost always come in the form of pills and never combine more than one remedy in one pill, anthroposophical medicines are also often administered by injection, while sometimes combinations of remedies are being used. Apart from prescribing medicines, anthroposophical doctors may also prescribe other therapeutic procedures, such as art or movement therapy (eurhythmy), based on anthroposophical principles. Anthroposophical doctors are always first trained in orthodox medicine before specializing in anthroposophical medicine.

The anthroposophical movement is not very widely represented in Great Britain, but it has a strong foothold and many followers in the rest of Europe, in particular in Germany, Switzerland — where in 1913 in a place called Dornach the world headquarters of the Anthroposophical Society were established — and in the Netherlands.

Anthroposophical medicine and children

Anthroposophy is a philosophy of life and of man's destiny in this world and so it holds strong views on the physical, mental, emotional and spiritual development of children.

Anthroposophical medicine was ahead of its time when it emphasized the relationship between a mother's diet and the health of the developing embryo and it has always been a great advocate of breast-feeding. It also has strong opinions on the diet of the developing child, arguing for instance that the introduction of too many animal proteins at too early an age may result in precocious development with undesirable consequences later on in the child's life.

Illness is seen as the manifestation of a disturbance in the harmony between the four components of the human being and illness in children is regarded as a sign of a necessary step in their development.

Much importance is therefore attributed to properly nursing a child through an illness rather than suppressing its symptoms.

Because it is presumed that there is such a close relationship between children's physical development and their mental, emotional, and spiritual development, medical advice is often combined with advice to parents on how to bring up their children, while older children are encouraged to become active participants in their own healing process and to adopt a change of lifestyle if necessary.

Anthroposophical medicine considers vaccination as a serious interference with the human organism, especially in the case of childhood diseases, and warns against vaccination as a routine procedure (see also page 33).

In countries where anthroposophical hospitals have been established, notably in Germany, some anthroposophical doctors have been able to specialize and have subsequently become consultants in paediatrics.

Further information
Francis X. King, *Rudolph Steiner and Holistic Medicine* (Century Hutchinson, 1986)
Wilhelm zur Linden, *A Child is Born* (Rudolf Steiner Press, 1980)
Petra Weeda, 'Antroposofische kindergeneeskunde', Jonas 7, 1987, pages 8-11
Anthroposophical Medical Association, Rudolf Steiner House, 35 Park Road, London NW1 6XT (tel: 01-723 4400)

Applied kinesiology and educational kinesiology

Applied kinesiology (pronounced kyn-easy-o-logy), or AK for short, is a system based on muscle testing by which it is possible to detect and correct imbalances in the body's energy flow. It was first developed by an American chiropractor, Dr George J. Goodheart in the mid 1960s. While practising chiropractic, he discovered that some muscles appeared to be weak, while they were not themselves atrophied, or withered. Further tests led to the observation that there are specific relationships between muscle weaknesses and certain organs and their functions. If a particular muscle is weak, the deficiency may be in any one of the associated energy systems, indicating a possible deficiency in associated organs or glands.

Goodheart's ideas were soon taken up by other chiropractors and applied kinesiology has become a fast-growing area in alternative health care.

The muscle tests are carried out by the practitioner holding the patient's arm or leg and assessing the amount of pressure the patient can exert. This way the practitioner gains information direct from the body and the test can identify imbalances, which can be on a structural/postural level, a chemical/nutritional level or a mental/emotional level. The muscle tests are also used to select which treatments will correct the imbalances and even to confirm the immediate effectiveness of treatment.

AK can be a very effective diagnostic tool

and it is increasingly being used as such by practitioners of various other therapies. The treatments used by practitioners of AK may vary somewhat from practitioner to practitioner, but can include chiropractic manipulation, light massage of body reflex points and acupuncture points (acupressure) and nutritional advice. Also relevant for treatment can be centering and coordination exercises and release of emotional stress.

The areas in which AK is most effective are relief of physical pain and tension, relief of emotional stress and discovery of individual reactions to foods. AK is also considered useful as a preventive therapy to increase energy and vitality.

Applied kinesiology and children

As AK is a very gentle procedure — both during diagnosis and treatment — it is very suitable for use with children from about seven upwards.

AK is considered particularly useful for children with allergy problems, but it has been suggested that all good preventive paediatric care should include AK muscle testing and evaluation. By detecting and correcting structural imbalances in the muscles and bones of a growing child, it would be possible to avoid chronic discomfort or pain in later life.

It has also been suggested that when children fall and severely bump their head, they should be checked by an AK practitioner for possible harmful consequences elsewhere in the body. Even if no symptoms develop straight away, the trauma caused by the fall may set off faulty nerve signals that can trigger symptoms of conditions at a later stage (see also chiropractic, page 96, and cranial osteopathy, page 107).

Self-help: Touch for health

Closely connected with applied kinesiology is touch for health. Its aim is to teach the skills of the professional kinesiologist to lay people so that they may use it to help themselves and their families. Touch for Health is advocated mainly as a tool for preventative health care.

Touch for health is often the first way someone encounters the scope and possibilities of applied kinesiology. It is not uncommon for someone to take a course on touch for health, then become a touch for health teacher and then train to become a practitioner of applied kinesiology. In the course of this career some people then decide to focus on one of the more specialized applications of AK, such as biokinesiology or educational kinesiology.

Educational kinesiology

One of the offshoots of AK is educational kinesiology (or edu-k for short), which helps people with coordination problems and learning difficulties, such as dyslexia. It was developed in the USA by educational expert Paul Dennison and has begun to reach a wider audience since the publication of his first book in 1981. Edu-k was introduced in Britain in 1986.

It appears that the enormous advances being made in brain research during the past few decades are now filtering through to psychological and educational experts. As a result, they are now in a much better

position to diagnose learning difficulties such as dyslexia and to devise ways of helping people who suffer from them. One such method is edu-k, which combines muscle testing techniques with simple exercises, referred to as 'Brain Gym'. Its aim is to promote better coordination of the two cerebral hemispheres, resulting in a more integrated use of eyes, ears and body. It is claimed that it is not only reading and spelling that can improve through edu-k, but all learning and creative activities.

The exercises are simple and natural movements, one of the most important of these being cross crawling. This is done in various ways — such as marching or skipping on the spot — but always in such a manner that when one arm moves, the leg on the opposite side of the body moves at the same time. The techniques being used also include some stretching exercises and touching of energy points, based on yoga exercises and acupuncture points. All activities are very simple to perform and can easily be fitted into a daily routine or used when the need is felt.

Edu-k can be carried out in the form of individual treatment, but the exercises can also be taught to groups of people. Conditions that are said to benefit most from edu-k are dyslexia, behavioural problems, balance problems and difficulties with concentration and coordination.

Educational kinesiology and children

Although edu-k can be used with adults, who find that they can make big improvements with regard to long-standing problems with reading or coordination, it is obviously even better to use it with children and to solve such problems at an early stage. However, because children have to be able to follow simple commands to carry out the exercises, it is easier to work with children who are not younger than seven or eight. Also, it is often not until around that age that a child will begin to become aware of any learning difficulties and his or her own motivation to change things will make edu-k more effective more quickly.

Self-help

The techniques and exercises used in edu-k are very simple and can easily be taught to parents so that they can use them with their children. When a child is treated by an edu-k practitioner on an individual basis, he or she will usually be given exercises to do at home. Also, edu-k is now being taught to groups of adults to use for themselves and their families.

Further information
Tom and Carol Valentine, *Applied Kinesiology* (Thorsons, 1985)
Paul E. Dennison, *Switching On*, A guide to edu-kinesthetics (Edu-kinesthetics, New York, 1981)
Paul E. Dennison and Gail E. Dennison, *Edu-k for Kids*! The basic manual on educational kinesiology for parents and teachers of kids of all ages (Edu-kinesthetics, California, 1987)
Paul E. Dennison and Gail E. Dennison, *Brain Gym*, Simple activities for whole brain learning (Edu-kinesthetics, California, 1986)
British Touch For Health Association, 29 Bushey Close, High Wycombe, Buckinghamshire, HP12 3HL (tel: 494 37409)

They can also supply information about applied kinesiology and educational kinesiology.

Bach flower remedies

The Bach flower remedies were developed by Dr Edward Bach (1880-1936), an English doctor who started his career as a pathologist and bacteriologist. Later in his life he became interested in homoeopathy and through his experiments with homoeopathic remedies he came to believe that remedies could be developed that would address themselves to the person rather than to the disease. By working directly on a person's emotional state, the remedies would help to relieve physical symptoms that are associated with that emotional state.

With the help of his own intuitive powers, Bach identified 38 wild flowers and trees from which he prepared his remedies. The method of preparation was strictly defined by Bach and is still being carried out according to his instructions at the Dr Edward Bach Centre, where his work has been preserved and continued since his death in 1936.

The most commonly used method for preparing the remedies is by infusion. This involves taking the blooms of the plant, floating them in a bowl of pure water and leaving them in bright sunshine for a few hours. Then the blossoms are removed and the water is poured into bottles to which some brandy is added to preserve the infusion. The resulting preparation is called the 'stock'. A few remedies are prepared by boiling in water the blossoms plus a piece of stem and some of the leaves from the plant. The liquid is then strained and made into stock.

The main function of the Bach flower remedies is to help the healing process. They are most often used in conjunction with other forms of treatment and are being prescribed by many different therapists such as acupuncturists, psychotherapeutic counsellors or indeed any other practitioner.

The Bach remedies have no side-effects and can be taken in combination with

The Bach flower remedies

Dr Bach divided his 38 remedies into seven groups covering various negative states of mind as listed below.

- Fear
  Rock rose
  Mimulus
  Cherry plum
  Aspen
  Red chestnut

- Uncertainty
  Cerato
  Scleranthus
  Gentian
  Gorse
  Hornbeam
  Wild oat

- Lack of interest in the present
  Clematis
  Honeysuckle
  Wild rose

- Despondency and despair
  Larch
  Pine
  Elm
  Sweet chestnut

  Star of Bethlehem
  Willow
  Oak
  Crab apple

- Over-care for the welfare of others
  Chicory
  Vervain
  Vine
  Beech
  Rock water
  Olive
  White chestnut
  Mustard
  Chestnut bud

- Loneliness
  Water violet
  Impatiens
  Heather

- Over-sensitivity
  Agrimony
  Centaury
  Walnut
  Holly

orthodox drugs or homoeopathic remedies.

The Bach remedies and children

The remedies are regarded as absolutely safe and can be given to children. As they are suitable for self-help and fairly easy to obtain, Bach flower remedies are quite popular among parents and it seems that using these remedies is quite often one of the first steps they take when beginning to explore alternative forms of medicine for their children.

As the Bach remedies are effective in transforming negative states of mind into positive attitudes, they can be particularly helpful when a child is going through a difficult phase. While for an adult, a negative state of mind can obviously be attributed to a multitude of reasons and causes, for children, especially young ones, it is more often possible to single out just one or a handful of causes or reasons. Examples are jealousy of a new-born sibling, for which Holly is recommended, and fear of darkness and nightmares, for which Aspen would be most suitable.

Self-help

The remedies are suitable for self-help and Dr Bach was himself a great advocate of self-help through his remedies. They can be bought at homoeopathic pharmacies, or can be ordered from the Dr Edward Bach Centre.

One of the most commonly used remedies is the Rescue Remedy (a standard mixture containing Rock Rose, Clematis, Impatiens, Cherry Plum and Star of Bethlehem), whether to relieve crying spells in babies or for first-aid treatment in small or major accidents. Even when it is obvious that urgent medical help is needed, giving the Rescue Remedy (either diluted in fruit juice or straight from the stock, moistening the lips with the remedy if the child is unconscious or is too distressed to swallow properly) can help the child's body to cope better with the shock when on the way to a doctor or the hospital.

For children and teenagers who have to take tests at school, a special Examination Mix is being recommended that helps the student to cope better with feelings of panic and fear of failure. The Examination Mix contains Clematis, Gentian and Larch, to which can be added Mimulus, Rock Rose or White Chestnut, depending on the child's character and needs. Unlike the Rescue Remedy, the Examination Mix cannot be bought ready-made, but it can be easily prepared at home.

Further information
Julian Barnard (Ed.), *Collected Writings of Edward Bach* (Bach Educational Programme, Hereford, 1987)
F.J. Wheeler, *The Bach Remedies Repertory* (The C.W. Daniel Company, 1988)
Edward Bach, *The Twelve Healers and Other Remedies* (The C.W. Daniel Company, 1988)
Gregory Vlamis, *Flowers to the Rescue* (Thorsons, 1986)
Dr Edward Bach Centre, Mount Vernon, Sotwell, Wallingford, Oxfordshire OX10 0PZ

Chiropractic

The practice of spinal manipulation can be traced back thousands of years and references to it can be found in old Greek and Chinese manuscripts. However, modern chiropractic was founded in the USA at the end of the nineteenth century by a healer called Daniel David Palmer (1845-1913), who discovered that, by working on a person's spine, he could heal conditions that were affecting other parts of the body.

During and after his lifetime the ideas of Palmer met with fierce opposition from practitioners of orthodox medicine, but this hasn't prevented chiropractors becoming one of the largest group of practitioners of health care, especially in the USA where there is one chiropractor for every 13,000 people.

These days chiropractors are regarded as specialists in diagnosing and treating disorders of the spine, joints and muscles. Conditions they treat most commonly are backaches, headaches and migraine, pains in the neck, shoulders or arms, sports injuries and stress. During treatment, a chiropractor makes specific adjustments to parts of the spine by manipulation, while the patient is standing, sitting or lying down on a specially designed chiropractic couch.

For lay people it is sometimes difficult to distinguish between chiropractic and osteopathy (see page 105) and it is true that both therapies do closely resemble each other. It seems that the differences are mainly historical and that, in recent years, both chiropractors and osteopaths have not only shown more tolerance towards

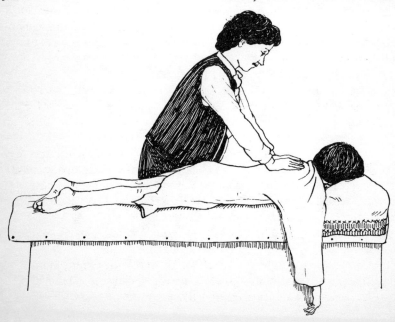

each other but have also become increasingly interested in each other's techniques.

A recent offshoot of chiropractic is applied kinesiology (see page 89) and some chiropractors now specialize in diagnosing and treating patients with principles based on AK.

Chiropractic and children

As chiropractic is most often associated with backaches and headaches, conditions that are not particularly prevalent amongst children, most chiropractors' patients are adults. However, chiropractic is also considered suitable for the treatment of children. The techniques being used are basically the same as those for adults, although extra care will be taken so that the manipulation is always very gentle and X-rays, a common form of diagnosis in chiropractic, will normally not be taken of children.

Conditions most commonly treated in children are birth traumas, infant colic, strains and muscle imbalances, scoliosis (curvature of the spine), injuries caused by falls and accidents and sports injuries, the latter resulting when children and teenagers feel compelled to do too much

too soon in competitive sports.

When working with children, chiropractors see it as their most important role to contribute to preventative health care. It is thought that many symptoms that occur in adult life can be traced back to some form of spinal injury in that person's early years. Also, bad postural habits caused by unsuitable chairs and school desks that are too low, may result in spinal problems that, when left uncorrected, can produce backaches and headaches in later years.

Early diagnosis and treatment of spinal distortions may prevent much trouble and it is therefore suggested by the chiropractic profession that parents should take their children for a chiropractic check-up in the same way as they take them to the dentist.

Further information
Anthea Courtenay, *Chiropractic for Everyone* (Penguin, 1987)
F. Sykes, 'Major considerations in chiropractic treatment of children and adolescents', *Bulletin of the European Chiropractors' Union*, 29, 1981, pages 27-33 British Chiropractic Association, 5 First Avenue, Chelmsford, Essex CM1 1RX (tel: 0245 358487)

Herbalism

Herbalism, the use of plants and herbs for healing purposes, has been practised by people all over the world and through the centuries. Knowledge about the medical qualities of particular plants has traditionally been handed down from

generation to generation, mostly orally. In England, the most famous written record of herbs was compiled by Nicholas Culpeper and dates from the seventeenth century. To this day Culpeper's name remains closely associated with herbalism and his book, *Culpeper's Complete Herbal*, is still available today.

Until fairly recently in human history, plants and herbs were the only forms of drugs available. However, with the advance of science and the development of synthetic drugs on a large scale, herbalism had become an all but extinct skill in the Western world, until the recent revival of interest in natural forms of medicine brought it back into practice.

Although herbal remedies are often used as an auxiliary therapy by naturopaths and other therapists, medical herbalism is to be considered a therapy in its own right that is first and foremost practised by trained medical herbalists. A medical herbalist diagnoses patients and prescribes herbal remedies, mostly in the form of tinctures. Herbalism, however, is considered a holistic therapy, which means that it does not just treat the symptoms but takes into account a person's whole lifestyle and, for this reason, herbalists will also often give their patients nutritional and other advice on healthy living. Some herbalists, in the tradition of their predecessors who practised medicine when herbs were the only drugs available, see themselves as general practitioners, treating the various members of whole families, rather than just individual patients.

Although herbalism can be effective in treating symptoms and is frequently used for that purpose, medical herbalists feel they have also an important role to play in preventive health care. By looking for imbalances in a person as an emotional and physiological being and by trying to

correct them, a herbalist can help someone to become a healthier person who is in a better position to fight and withstand illnesses when they occur.

Herbalism and children

Herbalism for children is essentially the same as herbalism for adults. The same remedies are used, albeit in less concentrated forms, and one of the advantages of using herbal tinctures for children is that they are very easy to take and are considered generally safe and free from side-effects. When a baby is being breast-fed, remedies will be given to the mother.

Herbalism doesn't offer an alternative to vaccination in the same way as homoeopathy (see page 100), but herbal remedies are available for the actual treatment of childhood illnesses such as measles, mumps and whooping cough, when they occur. Other conditions commonly treated by herbalists in children are colic, asthma and eczema, headaches, stomach aches and insomnia.

A medical herbalist will usually treat chronic or recurrent illnesses. In the case of acute conditions, such as meningitis, that need immediate orthodox treatment, herbalists feel they have a contribution to make by giving after-care, as they can prescribe herbal remedies that will build up the child's constitution.

Herbal remedies can be used effectively for self-help, but the advice of a trained medical herbalist can be of great value for chronic or recurrent conditions. For example, if a child has one occurrence of tonsillitis in two years, it can be treated by herbalism on a first-aid basis. However, a child with recurrent bouts of tonsillitis, would seem to have more of a constitutional problem and a trained herbalist could advise the parent on how to try to prevent the illness from happening so frequently.

Self-help

Every time you make a concoction of, for instance, lemon and cloves to nurse a cold, or drink herbal tea, or add some herb extracts to your bath water, it could be said that you are practising herbalism. Obviously this is only one (limited) aspect of what herbalism is about, but, even if you are consulting a medical herbalist, the actual treatment of the condition will take place at home, by taking the remedies (or administering them to your child) and following up nutritional or other therapeutic advice.

When a child is sick at home, a herbalist who knows the family from previous consultations will sometimes give advice over the phone on specific remedies to use and on general nursing care, thus helping you to help yourself and your family. Also, when you get familiar with certain herbs or remedies and how they work for you or your child, you can keep a supply of them at home — ranging from kitchen herbs such as thyme and rosemary to more specific medicinal herbs such as feverfew and marigold (calendula) — and use them when needed. These days, herbalism is being taught in courses directed at the general public, mostly concentrating on the first-aid aspect of herbal remedies, and these courses prove very popular especially with mothers.

Further information
David Hoffmann, *The Herb User's Guide* (Thorsons, 1987)
David Hoffmann, *The Holistic Herbal* (Element, 1983)
National Institute of Medical Herbalists, PO Box 3, Winchester, Hampshire (tel: 0962 68776)

Homoeopathy

Homoeopathy is a system of medicine that was founded in the early nineteenth century by a German doctor called Samuel Hahnemann and is based on the principle 'let like be cured with like'. In other words, a substance that produces symptoms of sickness in a healthy person can cure similar symptoms in a sick person.

Using himself as a guinea-pig, Hahnemann began his experiments by taking quinine, the traditional medicine for treating malaria, and noticed that it produced in him the symptom of malaria. He thus discovered that when a medicine was given to a healthy person, it produced the symptoms of the disease it was aimed to cure. From the numerous tests, or provings as he called them, he carried out on himself and on volunteers, he postulated that the symptoms of a disease are in fact the symptoms of the body resisting that particular disease. The homoeopathic medicines, or remedies as they are called, he developed were therefore aimed at triggering the body's own defence mechanism rather than at suppressing the symptoms, as is the case with most allopathic drugs (drugs used in orthodox medicine).

Homoeopathic preparations are made from substances of vegetable, mineral or animal origin. The substances are diluted hundreds, thousands or even millions of times by a special method that involves vigorous shaking, or succussion. The resulting dilutions are known as potencies and the numbers they are given indicate the number of times a substance has been diluted. Because the remedies are given in such highly diluted doses, they do not produce any side-effects.

From the beginning, acceptance of homoeopathy by the orthodox medical profession has been mostly negative, varying from outright hostile reactions to more covert opposition. Among the general public, however, there have always been devoted followers and users, although their numbers have varied considerably over the years, and nowadays homoeopathy is considered one of the most established forms of alternative medicine.

Until fairly recently most homoeopathic doctors were first trained in orthodox medicine, but there are now growing numbers of homoeopaths who have not first received orthodox medical training but whose medical training is incorporated in their training in homoeopathic medicine. Also, an increasing number of alternative practitioners make use of homoeopathic remedies as a complement to their own particular therapy.

Homoeopathy and children

It is generally accepted that homoeopathic remedies, as they don't have any side-effects, can safely be used in the treatment of children of all ages. Many homoeopaths treat all the members of a family, thus practising as a family doctor.

As homoeopathic treatment concerns itself not just with the disease but with the whole person, there is a long list of remedies to choose from for each condition. It is sometimes argued that homoeopathic prescribing is actually easier for children than it is for adults. The reason for this would be that, for a correct prescription, a person's whole life-style needs to be taken into account and for a child the circumstances are usually less complicated than for an adult. On the other hand, it is argued that children also suffer from fear, anxiety and other emotional traumas and only if all their physical, emotional and mental symptoms are taken into account can successful prescribing take place.

In the case of very young children, who cannot describe their own symptoms, it is obvious that the observations of practitioners and parents become very important. However, children who are regularly treated with homoeopathy will learn to give precise answers to the detailed questions being asked by a homoeopath and they can become quite skilful at describing what is bothering them from an early age.

Homoeopathic treatment is used for all common childhood conditions, from nappy rash to earache, from infant colic to tonsillitis. Homoeopathic remedies are also used to treat infectious childhood illnesses such as mumps, measles and whooping cough. Not only are remedies available for when these illnesses occur, there are also remedies that are considered an alternative to vaccination.

When it comes to vaccination, homoeopathy has various procedures on offer:

● you can use a homoeopathic antidote to an orthodox vaccine when there has been a bad reaction to a vaccination that has already been given

● you can use homoeopathic preparations instead of orthodox vaccines

● you can use constitutional treatment to raise the child's resistance to disease

● you can use homoeopathic remedies to treat the illness if it occurs.

As homoeopathic treatment is always geared towards each individual person, it is important to realize that the best procedure for one child may not necessarily be the right one for another. Moreover, individual homoeopathic practitioners prefer some methods to others and if you want to consider homoeopathic treatment as an alternative to vaccination, it is therefore of utmost importance that you find an experienced homoeopathic practitioner and discuss the various options with him or her.

Homoeopathic remedies address themselves to the patient as a complete psychological and physical being and so they are also prescribed for emotional disturbances and illnesses. In the case of children and teenagers, some problems that can be treated by homoeopathic prescribing are tantrums, jealousy, insecurity and fear, hyperactivity, school phobias, clumsiness, depression and anorexia nervosa.

Self-help

Homoeopathy is suitable for self-help and remedies can be freely bought in homoeopathic pharmacies, health food shops and so on. It seems that homoeopathy is becoming increasingly popular among parents to use for their children for minor disturbances such as colds and stomach upsets. As it is necessary to know the whole person for homoeopathic prescribing, parents seem to be in an excellent position to prescribe quite precisely for their own children, knowing them intimately as they do, although there is of course a risk of being too closely involved and therefore not being able to be sufficiently objective. Occasional consultations with a practitioner should help a parent to check their observations against those of someone less involved.

> *Before you consider prescribing remedies for your child, it is advisable to find out more about homoeopathy and the principles it is based upon. Some homoeopathic colleges, clinics or practitioners now run first-aid courses where parents can learn how to treat their children and this is a good starting point.*

Most homoeopathic practitioners encourage self-help and even supply their patients with a first-aid kit, sometimes tailor-made for a particular patient or family. Also, homoeopaths are often prepared to give advice over the phone to their regular patients. There are also many homoeopathic handbooks available describing the remedies for the most common illnesses.

Listing your remedies

As there are so many different remedies to choose from (there are over 2,000 different remedies, but obviously some are used more frequently than others) it is impossible to have them all at home yourself. It can be a good idea, therefore, to make a list of the remedies you keep at home and exchange it with one or two friends who also use homoeopathic remedies and who live not too far away. That way you have a much larger range of remedies to choose from, which can be very helpful especially during evenings and at weekends.

Further information

American Homeopathy, vol. 2, no. 3, March, 1985 — the whole issue is on homoeopathy for children
'Immunizations: Do they protect our children?', *American Homeopathy,* vol. 1 no. 2, September, 1984, page 9
Leon Chaitow, *Vaccination and Immunization: Dangers, Delusions and Alternatives,* What every parent should know (The C.W. Daniel Company, 1987)
Trevor Smith, *The Homoeopathic Treatment of Emotional Illness,* A self-help guide to remedies which can restore calm and happiness (Thorsons, 1983)
Phyllis Speight, *Homoeopathic Remedies for Children* (The C.W. Daniel Company, 1983)
British Homoeopathic Association, 27a Devonshire Street, London W1N 1RJ (tel: 01-935 2163)
Society of Homoeopaths, 2 Artizan Road, Northampton NN1 4HU (tel: 0604 21400)

Hypnotherapy

Most alternative therapies work on a physical level even though the holistic approach involves taking into account the psychological aspects of illness. Some therapies, however, work only through the patient's psyche and one of these is hypnotherapy or hypnosis.

For many people, the word hypnosis is mostly linked with the dubious practice of putting people into a sort of half-sleep so that they obey any command given to them by the hypnotist. This kind of 'stage hypnotism', however, represents only a tiny fraction of the range of possible uses of hypnosis.

There is nothing mysterious or magical about hypnosis. We have all noticed from time to time in ourselves or in someone else that sensation of being 'miles away' or 'in another world', and in this sense the hypnotic state is part of our normal, everyday life. One way to describe the hypnotic state is as an area between sleep on the one hand and conscious awareness on the other and when an individual's awareness of his or her surroundings is diminished, while awareness of internal processes, feelings, thoughts and pictures is increased, one could say that he or she is in a hypnotic state. How someone reaches this state may vary from person to person, but a hypnotherapist is someone who is trained to help you to reach it more quickly.

Suggestion plays an important part in hypnosis. Again there is nothing mysterious about this, for suggestion is also something that is very much part of our everyday life. When an idea or belief is being suggested to us several times *and* we act upon it, the resulting act may become part of our behaviour. In itself there is nothing wrong with acting upon an idea in a set pattern — we do it ourselves all the time and it is also basically the way we bring up our children — unless the pattern is a maladjusted or a self-defeating one. Hypnosis can help to change someone's particular pattern of response by uncovering the initial suggestion that triggered the response and helping the person to choose a more productive one. Well-known and obvious examples are smoking and obesity, where a patient's compulsive pattern to smoke or to eat can be changed for a pattern of a more relaxed response to situations of stress.

Hypnosis or hypnotherapy has probably been practised by people throughout the world and throughout the centuries. Modern hypnosis can be traced back to the late eighteenth century, when an Austrian physician called Franz Mesmer invented a form of 'animal magnetism'.

This early form of hypnotherapy was consequently developed by followers of his and was particularly used in conjunction with pain relief. The present interest in using hypnosis for many different medical purposes, including dentistry, dates back about 25 to 30 years.

Hypnotherapists can be doctors, dentists or psychologists, but there are also non-medically trained therapists.

Self-hypnosis

Another form of hypnosis is self-hypnosis, or autohypnosis, during which people bring about the hypnotic state themselves through deep relaxation. Some hypno-therapists teach self-hypnosis to their patients so that they can then practise at home between visits to the therapist.

Hypnotherapy and children

It is said that, as a rule, children make very good hypnotic subjects. Conditions in children treated most commonly with hypnotherapy include asthma, bed-wetting, nail-biting, exam nerves, migraine, obesity, stammering, eczema, and emotional disturbances, and it has also been used successfully during dental treatment. Moreover, any reasonably intelligent child of nine years or more can learn self-hypnosis or autohypnosis. In a research project carried out by Dr Maher-Loughnan, testing the use of autohypnosis for the treatment of a wide variety of psychosomatic conditions, it was found that patients under the age of 20 responded more quickly.

To practise autohypnosis on a regular basis, however, a child will need to have a good reason for doing it — for instance, having bad attacks of migraine — otherwise he or she will get bored with it and won't do it. Children like to be active and to run around, and autohypnosis means they have to become quiet and calm.

Another form of hypnotherapy that has been developed by an American doctor, Milton Erickson, is called 'indirect hypnosis'. This form of hypnosis uses stories containing suggestions that are useful for a particular person or problem. The most convenient way is to put a story on tape that can then be listened to at home. As most children like listening to stories and often don't mind hearing the same tape over and over again, this can be a particularly suitable form of treatment for them.

Further information
Steven Heller and Terry Steele, *Monsters and Magical Sticks* (Falcon Press, Phoenix, 1987)
J.B. Wilkinson, 'Hypnotherapy in the psychosomatic approach to illness: a review', *Journal of the Royal Society of Medicine* vol. 74, July, 1981
The British Society of Medical and Dental Hypnosis, 42 Links Road, Ashtead, Surrey KT21 2HT (tel: 03722 73522)

Metamorphics

The founder of the metamorphic technique, or metamorphics, was Robert St John, who developed the technique in the 1960s through his work as a naturopath and reflexologist. Although originally based on reflexology (see page 46), the method used in metamorphics and the results obtained are now considered completely different.

Metamorphics is based on the belief that many predispositions to illness can be traced back to the prenatal period, an idea that is beginning to gain ground amongst other health care professionals as well. The various stages of the prenatal period correspond with certain areas on the foot, and it is by pressing the relevant points that the healing process can be set in motion. Although most attention is paid to the feet, practitioners of metamorphics also work on the head and hands of a patient.

A treatment session will usually last for one hour and will take place on a weekly basis. Apart from being a therapy in its own right, it also has a place as being a part of or an adjunct to other forms of treatment.

Metamorphics and children
Many of the early patients of Robert St John were children with disabilities, as he found that these children were particularly amenable to the treatment and, although metamorphics is now used to treat patients of all ages and with all sorts of conditions, it is still often used to treat children. Success is particularly claimed for children with developmental disorders, including children suffering from brain damage and Down's syndrome.

Self-help

Metamorphics is suitable for self-help and it is actually believed that treatment is more effective if the entire family is involved rather than just the person to be treated. Apart from giving treatment, a practitioner will therefore also usually teach parents how to massage their children's feet at home. There are, in fact, several instances on record of parents who had first taken up metamorphics to treat a child of their own and who subsequently trained to become professional therapists (see also page 74).

Further information
Gaston St Pierre and Debbie Boater, *The Metamorphic Technique* (Element, 1982)
Metamorphic Association, 67 Ritherden Road, London SW17 8QE (tel: 01-672 5951)

Naturopathy

While the origins of some therapies can be dated back to a certain time and person, it could be argued that naturopathic medicine or naturopathy, which relies primarily on natural agents such as water and fresh air, exercise and rest, and healthy foods and drinks, is as old as human history. Not only did the Greeks and Romans use naturopathy, but many people did so before them and have done so since.

Although in the nineteenth century there was considerable interest in naturopathic ideas, the growth and success of modern drugs in the twentieth century seemed to make the approach of naturopathy a slow and old-fashioned one. In recent years, however, there has been an important revival of naturopathic ideas and methods, in line with the growing interest in natural methods and treating the whole person rather than just a specific disease.

Naturopaths are primarily interested in preventive health care and they consider that one of their main tasks is to be educators in health and to help their patients achieve an optimum level of well-being, both in body and in mind. Although you visit a naturopath at a practice, most of the actual treatment will take place at home, for instance by having to follow a particular diet or by applying hydrotherapy (water compresses, hot and cold baths). Naturopathy is also practised at residential clinics, traditionally at or near spas. Modern naturopathic establishments are now often known as 'health farms'.

During a consultation, a naturopath will take a patient's medical history and carry out a physical examination, sometimes including diagnostic techniques such as iridology (a method of diagnosis by which information is obtained by studying a patient's iris). A naturopath can also do further investigations, such as blood tests or urine analysis.

The practitioner will then decide which level (structural/postural, biochemical/nutritional or mental/emotional) the patient needs help and in what way intervention should take place to restore the body's natural balance. Apart from using strictly naturopathic methods, many naturopaths prescribe herbal remedies and may also use other therapies, the most common ones being osteopathy and acupuncture.

Naturopathy and children

Naturopathic care is considered very suitable for children as the body's own healing power is particularly strong in a growing child. Also, the importance of a special diet for particular disorders in children such as asthma, eczema or hyperactivity, which has always been advocated by naturopaths, is now more generally recognized.

In line with the naturopathic philosophy of preventive health care and treating the whole person, a naturopath will try to achieve an overall improvement in a child's state of health. A naturopath would stress, for instance, that the right course of action is not to overprotect a child, but to make him or her more sturdy through exercise and sport, with the aim of making the child more resistant to disease.

Conditions in children that are treated most commonly by naturopaths are eczema and other skin problems, asthma and other respiratory disorders, allergies, behavioural problems and gastrointestinal disorders. Naturopractic practitioners will treat children of all ages. Some of them function as a 'family doctor' and will have seen all or most members of a family at various points of time.

Self-help

Naturopathy is very suitable for self-help and naturopaths will frequently teach their patients how to apply certain naturopathic methods at home. Examples are the use of water compresses, hot and cold baths, the use of vitamins and herbal remedies and, of course, following a special diet. A lot of traditional nursing care is, in fact, based on naturopathic principles, such as lots of fluids for a feverish child and sponging a child with lukewarm water to lower the temperature.

As so much of naturopathic treatment takes place at home, it takes a certain commitment by the parent who looks after the child. Also, as a child gets older, he or she will have to be convinced of the necessity of the treatment. Keeping to a strict diet, for example, is not always easy and a child might find it easier to use orthodox medication than not eat certain foods.

Further information
Roger Newman Turner, *Naturopathic Medicine*, Treating the whole person (Thorsons, 1984)
British Naturopathic and Osteopathic Association, 6 Netherhall Gardens, London NW3 5RR (tel: 01-435 8728)

Osteopathy and cranial osteopathy

Osteopathy was first developed as a system of healing in the USA in the second half of the nineteenth century by Dr Andrew Taylor Still. It is based on the belief that structure governs function and that a sound structure of the body is essential for good health. Consequently, osteopathy works on the principle that many disorders can be treated by realigning structural deviations.

In osteopathic treatment, particular attention is paid to the spinal cord, for it is believed that, as an extension of the brain, it controls all bodily functions. Correct alignment of the spine will therefore not only relieve back pain, the most common complaint for which people go to an osteopath, but will also ensure proper functioning of vital organs such as the heart, liver and lungs.

Osteopathic treatment consists of manipulating various parts of the body as well as working on soft tissue.

Cranial osteopathy

In the 1930s the principles of cranial osteopathy were put forward by Dr William Sutherland, an American

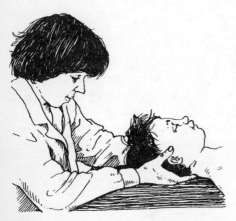

osteopath who for many years had studied the human skull. One of his discoveries was that there is movement between the twenty-two bones of the skull. He also found out how this movement and possible blocks to the motion could produce symptoms elsewhere in the body. As an outcome of his research, Sutherland established cranial osteopathy, regarding it as an extension and further development of the teachings of Andrew Taylor Still.

During treatment, the practitioner feels for the cerebro-spinal fluid and its rhythm or pulse, which gets transmitted throughout the body but can be felt especially keenly on the cranium (skull) and at the base of the spine. Any distortions in this rhythm can point to blocked movement between the bones of the skull. By feeling this cranio-sacral pulse and by applying very slight pressure to it, the practitioner can adjust the pulse and bring about changes that can resolve symptoms elsewhere in the body.

Osteopathy, cranial osteopathy and children

Although osteopathy has sometimes been associated with 'bone-cracking' techniques, which don't seem to make it a suitable therapy to use with children, it can actually be a gentle procedure, geared to the needs of each patient.

Osteopathic treatment for children usually involves very little manipulation and cranial osteopathy is one of the forms of treatment commonly used. As treatment by cranial osteopathy is always very gentle, it has been proven very suitable for diagnosing and treating certain conditions in children. Babies from only a few hours old can be treated as well as toddlers, older children and adolescents.

Cranial osteopathy can be effective in the treatment of babies and infants for birth injuries that have been caused by a difficult birth, the use of forceps or vacuum extraction. Even after a normal birth, however, cranial osteopaths advise parents to have their babies checked for any birth strain patterns, as a compression of the infantile head received during birth may persist and not be naturally resolved. This is especially the case when the baby is born premature and the head is still too soft, or postmature and the head is already too hard.

Unresolved birth strain patterns may lead to a variety of clinical symptoms and conditions that are commonly treated by cranial osteopaths and these can include infant colic, hyperactivity and behavioural problems, recurrent colds, coughs and asthma. While growing up, a child may receive a major knock that can lead to a compression similar to that of a birth injury. This is why cranial osteopaths feel that a child should be checked after a nasty fall or bump on the head, after falling down the stairs or off a bike or horse, for example, especially if the child's behaviour seems to have changed since the accident.

It is also thought to be advisable to have children checked by a cranial osteopath when they are having orthodontic treatment and, in fact, recently some dentists have started to become interested in the possibility of using cranial osteopathy to prevent and correct problems with children's jaws.

Teenagers can benefit from osteopathic treatment if they are involved in a lot of sporting activities or when they are experiencing a growth spurt. When growing fast, the body has to make new adjustments and during this process earlier traumas, caused by falls or injuries, may be uncovered and may start to cause trouble. Physical pains in an adolescent, such as recurrent backaches, should never be dismissed as simply growing pains, but should be checked and, if necessary, treated by an osteopath.

Further information
Chris Belshaw, *Osteopathy, Is it for you?* (Element, 1987)
British Naturopathic and Osteopathic Association, 6 Netherhall Gardens, London NW3 5RR (tel: 01-435 8728)
The General Council and Register of Osteopaths, 21 Suffolk Street, London SW1Y 4HG (tel: 01-839 2060)

Rolfing

The originator of Rolfing or structural integration was Dr Ida Rolf, an American biochemist and physiologist. Although she developed her ideas and methods in the 1930s and 1940s, it wasn't until the 1960s that they first gained wider recognition.

Dr Rolf's basic assumption was that the body's balance and movement can be improved by manipulating the body's connective tissue and muscle, those tissues

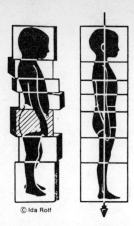

© Ida Rolf

that hold the skeleton together. Dr Rolf viewed the body as being rather like a tower of bricks that, if everything is well, are neatly stacked upon each other with each block resting on the one below. If, however, one brick, or part of the body, gets misaligned, the whole structure tends to get out of balance. Other parts of the body will adjust and compensate for the block that is out of alignment to regain a new balance, but, in doing so, often become misaligned themselves. The purpose of Rolfing is to restore the 'tower of bricks' to its proper structure.

A course of Rolfing therapy usually consists of ten hourly sessions. It is not uncommon for a practitioner to take photographs before and after treatment so that differences in posture can be easily spotted. Various massage techniques are used to 'free' or loosen the soft tissues of the body. The outcome of a course of Rolfing therapy is not only an improved posture, but also a general enhancement of physical and emotional well-being.

Rolfing and children

Ida Rolf herself was very interested in working with children, as she believed that corrections to posture can and should be made before bad postural habits start producing problems. It is argued that structural work is both corrective and preventive and that the earlier structural abnormalities in a child are being dealt with, the more chances there are that they can be overcome.

Practitioners of Rolfing also stress the relationship between physical and emotional well-being. It is pointed out that if a child slumps physically, he or she will also slump mentally and emotionally. Conversely, a child whose body is balanced and who moves gracefully and confidently reflects an inner grace and confidence.

Although for adults treatment is not always painless, in the case of children manipulation will be a very gentle and playful process and, as children's bodies are still supple, they are more amenable to the changes being brought about. Conditions treated most often are club foot, flat feet, strange styles of walking, breathing difficulties and postural and movement problems.

Further information
Thomas Myers, 'Rolfing for children', *Human Potential Resources*, vol. 9, no. 4, page 4
Thomas Myers, 'The "ideal" body', *Human Potential Resources*, vol. 10, no. 2, page 13
Robert Toporek, *The Promise of Rolfing*

Children (Transformation News Network, Philadelphia, 1981)

Dr Ida P. Rolf, *Rolfing* (Harper & Row, New York, 1977)

The Rolfing Network, 61 Grantham Road, London W4 2RT (tel: 01-994 8544)

Shiatsu

Shiatsu is a traditional Japanese massage technique. Its foundations probably date back thousands of years, but it wasn't named as an individual technique, distinguished from other forms of massage, until the beginning of this century. Although the word 'shiatsu' means finger pressure, the hands, elbows, knees and even feet are used in shiatsu to apply pressure to various parts of the body.

Shiatsu recognizes the same meridians that are used in acupuncture and the healing power of shiatsu is based on the belief that, by applying pressure to various points along the meridians, the body's vital energy (or ki) can be balanced and restored. It is therefore sometimes referred to as acupressure.

Although a fairly recent import to the West, it is quickly gaining popularity as a pleasurable and effective way of releasing tension and replacing lost energy. It is used for pain relief and is also considered relevant for some chronic disorders such as migraine and constipation, by preventing too much tension and stress building up in the body, and this is its main application when it is used for self-help.

One treatment session lasts for up to one hour and usually people begin by coming on a weekly basis. Gradually the time span between sessions will increase, but often people keep coming back on a regular basis for preventive treatment.

Shiatsu and children

Shiatsu is considered useful in treating children, because it doesn't require needles as acupuncture does and, because the practitioner works with direct touch, he or she can adapt the amount of pressure being used to the needs of each individual child, which gives shiatsu a gentle and human character. It is often found that children like having shiatsu and that older children can also be taught some self-help techniques.

It is argued that shiatsu appears to work well for children because they have less preconceived ideas about how energy, or ki, works or, as one practitioner put it, 'They haven't decided yet that they don't have energy lines in their bodies.' Also, more children are now familiar with oriental martial arts such as karate, which

is also based on the use and focusing of energy, and it can be easily explained to them that shiatsu works with the same energy, albeit in a somewhat different way.

Shiatsu treatment for children can be beneficial for conditions caused by tension or structural problems, for example migraine, breathing difficulties, insomnia and stammering.

Shiatsu massage can also be given to babies and toddlers, when it involves gentle stroking rather than using pressure, and it is said that when parents learn to use it with their own children both they and their children will benefit from it.

Self-help

Shiatsu is always given on a one-to-one basis and, in the case of specific complaints, treatment by a trained practitioner is the best procedure. However,

shiatsu is also suitable for self-help and is now being taught to groups where people are instructed how to work on each other. Basic knowledge of shiatsu involves being familiar with the position of the meridians and how to work on them in a gentle way.

Closely related to shiatsu are exercises similar to those used in yoga that are designed to stretch the meridians. They are called *makko ho* and a shiatsu therapist will often advise patients to do some of these at home in between shaitsu treatments at a practice.

Further information
Wataru Ohashi with Mary Hoover, *Touch for Love*, Shiatsu for your baby (Ballantine Books, New York, 1985)
Shiatsu Society, 19 Langside Park, Kilbarchan, Renfrewshire PA10 2EP (tel: 05057 4657)

CHAPTER SEVEN
Case histories

One of the questions frequently asked when alternative forms of health care are being discussed is 'What proof is there that these methods of preventative health care and the alternative treatment of illness really work?'

Over many, many years, lots of people — therapists as well as patients — have testified to the effectiveness of alternative medicine. There is an abundance of anecdotal reports and case histories, both published and in the files of therapists, that describe effective forms of preventative health care as well as successful treatment of a great variety of conditions.

As can be seen from the ever increasing numbers of people consulting alternative therapists the general public seems to accept these anecdotes and case histories as sufficient proof of the effectiveness of alternative forms of medicine. After all, the majority of practitioners get the majority of their patients by word of mouth, which would seem to indicate that people believe each other's accounts of their own successful use of alternative medicine.

A book on alternative medicine is therefore hardly complete without some case histories demonstrating to the reader the effective workings of the therapy or therapies described in the book. However, as most books on alternative health care are written by practitioners of alternative therapies, the case histories presented are usually those of successful cases, with the main focus on particular symptoms and the treatment given. The case histories presented in this book focus rather more on the 'search for healing' of the parents and children concerned, the choices they have made and their successful or sometimes not so successful dealings with both the orthodox and the alternative medical worlds.

With the exception of one that was provided by a therapist, all the case histories were obtained directly from the parents (in all the cases it was in fact the mothers) although in a few cases the contact with a particular parent was established via a practitioner.

I feel that these case histories may prove

to be as useful to those of you using or contemplating using alternative medicine for their children as the rest of the book put together! It is certainly true that I learned as least as much from the parents I talked to as from the practitioners I consulted or from the books I read.

Infant's colic

‘ When my baby was about three months old, she was crying an awful lot and had never once slept through the night. The only thing that seemed to comfort her was sucking and I resorted to using a dummy as well as putting her to the breast every couple of hours.

Both the health visitor and the doctor said it was colic and that she would grow out of it, but my nerves were growing thin. I'll try anything once, so I went to a cranial osteopath.

Was the birth traumatic? Not for me, so it hadn't occurred to me at first that her crying could have something to do with that. The second stage of the birth had been very long, however, and the continued pressure had brought up a bump on her head. This must have upset the pulses in her head, as one was found to be out of line on the left-hand side of her head.

After just one session of very gentle pressure on the head by the cranial osteopath, my baby slept through the night for the first time and seemed altogether much happier. I myself had forgotten what sleep was like!

Also corrected was her lazy eyelid, which also linked up to the same trapped nerve. Just one more session was needed to make sure everything was back to normal and she now seems fine. It was definitely worth paying for the peace and quiet we get now! ’

Whooping cough

‘ My son was just nine months old when he suffered from a snotty nose, runny eyes and a slight cough. In addition, he was very fragile, cried a lot and couldn't cope with any frustration, and there was a lot around as he was starting to walk. At night he slept even worse than usual. Since he didn't seem to get any better after two or three days, I took him to be seen by a herbalist.

The herbalist took a very detailed history, examined his ears, throat and chest, and prescribed a medicine to be taken three times a day. For the next three days, my son seemed much the same during the day, maybe a bit more grizzly and he had stopped trying to walk. Very rapidly, though, his cough progressed to being much worse at night, when he would wake up with a hacking cough. During the third night, the cough developed into a proper attack, consisting of a series of coughs with his face bright red and eyes slightly bulging outwards from the strain and effort involved. When listening carefully, I could hear him draw in his breath in a laboured way and he then was actually whooping.

That same night I spoke to the herbalist on the phone, described the changes and mentioned that the initial symptoms and their subsequent development seemed consistent with whooping cough. Although I hoped to be told otherwise, she agreed with me. We therefore arranged another appointment for the following day.

In the morning my son coughed so badly while having breakfast that he vomited up all he had just eaten. He seemed exhausted and yet agitated and, just looking at him, it was obvious that he had become quite ill. By now I was convinced he could only have whooping cough, having spent half the night reading up on it. During the consultation with the herbalist, we again discussed all the changes and symptoms. He was examined again and then prescribed a different herbal medicine to account for the changed situation.

For about a day and a half he vomited at almost every meal, cried a lot and woke up at night due to the coughing attacks. And then, quite suddenly, he improved rapidly: he kept all his food down, coughed less severely and no longer woke up with every cough. He was generally less agitated and much happier within himself.

However, before life could return to normal, my son had to be seen by a GP, since Social Services require a medical certificate for all children suffering from a highly infectious or notifiable disease before they can attend any of their facilities again. Having explained what I had come for, the doctor proceeded to examine only his chest and no abnormal respiratory sounds were noted. She asked me why I thought it had been whooping cough. I described the course of his illness and again the diagnosis was confirmed.

Expressing her surprise at my son's fast recovery, she asked whether he had received any treatment. Because of past negative experiences in similar situations, I was very hesitant, but decided to tell her, since there was nothing to lose now. Her final comment was that he had made the best recovery from whooping cough she had come across in her practice, adding that the worst cases she had ever seen were her own (vaccinated) children. All in all, within two weeks after seeing the herbalist for the first time, my son stopped coughing altogether, picked himself up and walked.

Never during the time my son suffered from whooping cough did I have any doubt that herbal treatment was the right approach for him, nor did I regret my decision against vaccination. If anything, this episode strengthened my commitment to herbal medicine. ’

Cerebral palsy

‘ We were told that our son had cerebral palsy when he was 11 months old. From the beginning we were determined to be as involved as possible in whatever treatment would benefit him. It felt right to both of us to turn to alternative medicine in those early days in our quest to help our son. We had both used osteopathy, homoeopathy and the Alexander technique with considerable success and I had given our son Bach's rescue remedy from the time he was very little. On the whole, I felt confident in my own ability to know when I could rely on alternative medicine and when orthodox medicine was necessary.

We heard about cranial osteopathy from a newspaper article. We knew our son had had a traumatic birth, being two months premature and delivered with forceps, and, in the article, cranial osteopathy claimed to treat the damage done by traumatic birth.

We were given the name of a practitioner by someone who was training to become a cranial osteopath himself. We went for about ten weekly sessions, but I could see no change. Since I had not used cranial osteopathy myself, I had no firm expectations, but I did not expect immediate or dramatic results. I was patient to give the practitioner a reasonable length of time as long as he felt he was helping and our son was not objecting. What I found very worrying, however, was the practitioner's obvious lack of knowledge of basic milestones in infant development. He seemed unaware that a year-old boy who is still unable to roll over or crawl was in any way out of the ordinary. He just kept commenting on what a lovely smile our son had. He also questioned the diagnosis of cerebral palsy, which I felt was very unhelpful. From my own reading I was certain our son had cerebral palsy and the physiotherapy centre where we took him, which specialized in children with cerebral palsy, also felt confident in the diagnosis.

In short, I felt angry that the practitioner, who seemed to have little practical experience of babies with cerebral palsy, was holding out cranial osteopathy as "the answer" for our son. The sessions were expensive and I felt the practitioner's motives were suspect, although he seemed to be highly regarded by his profession.

Fortunately, since then we have had positive experiences using alternative medicine for our son. When he developed croup at age two, homoeopathy helped a great deal to relieve the coughing. It wasn't always able to prevent us having to go to hospital, but we could see results on the whole. We also used homoeopathy during several childhood illnesses and for stomach upsets, overexposure to the sun, fever, etc. After an operation for a squint, we gave him Arnica straight away and he recovered amazingly quickly.

We decided not to have our son immunized and were supported in this by our GP. He did have whooping cough and measles at ages four and five and we used homoeopathic treatment in both, but neither illness was severe. On the whole, I have used homoeopathy for our son the same way I do for myself: as a first choice for many conditions, but if symptoms seem worrying or persistent, I would consult my GP.

We have also tried reflexology and the Alexander technique to help alleviate the extreme stiffness and spasticity he has from his cerebral palsy. Neither of these methods, however, has had any long-term effect. The reflexologist was inexperienced in working with a child with a physical disability and after a few sessions she felt she had nothing to offer apart from the obvious pleasure our son experienced during the sessions. However, I have known children less severely affected by cerebral palsy who have found reflexology helpful. The Alexander teacher had wonderful intentions, but didn't understand the nature of severe spasticity. She overstretched his Achilles tendon, causing soreness for several weeks.

During all our forays into alternative medicine, we have remained philosophical about the experiences. No one has done any irreparable damage and, in several cases, our lives have all been made easier by our efforts. For us it has been important to feel we have not looked at our son's difficulty with a narrow approach but have tried different possibilities. In the process we have acquired a greater understanding of what we can and can't do for our son. We have also tried not to lose track of the fact that he is first and foremost a child with all the health needs any child has *as well as* having a physical disability. We would have used alternative medicine for him if he hadn't had cerebral palsy, so we are clear that our use of various therapies has been vital as we all attempt to live in "the normal world". ❯

Asthma

❮ When my daughter was about 16 months old, she started having attacks of wheezing. I took her to the GP, who told me she was suffering from asthma. He prescribed her some medicine and said that the only thing we could do, apart from taking the medicine, was learn to live with it.

I didn't like her being labelled as an asthmatic child and decided not to just accept it, but instead to find out whether there was anything else I could do for her. I took her to a homoeopath, who started by taking a very long and detailed case history. One of the things he mentioned was that her immune system had probably been weakened by the fact that I had had a whole lot of vaccinations just before I got pregnant, plus the vaccinations she had been given as a baby.

He prescribed remedies that were meant to build her up constitutionally and also a remedy to control wheezing if it occurred.

He also gave some dietary advice and said that, apart from not having dairy products, for which she had shown an intolerance since she was a small baby, she should avoid oranges, tomatoes and strawberries, but have some extra cinnamon with her food. Finally, he recommended that I get some psychological counselling, which I did, as he felt that my daughter's health problems had some connection with the problems I was having myself at the time.

We continued to see the same homoeopath about every three months for the next two years and all that time she was fine. She had very few wheezing attacks and, if they occurred, they could be controlled with homoeopathic remedies. And we never went to a GP during that period for, apart from the occasional wheezing and some minor illnesses, she was a very healthy child.

We then stopped seeing the homoeopath for a while and later found out that he had died. I am now building up a relationship with a new homoeopath, who practises in a local health centre. Lately, my daughter, who is now six years old, has been wheezing a little more often than usual, but I still feel it can be controlled by using homoeopathic remedies and to this day she has never used any inhalers or other allopathic medicines for it.)

Ear trouble and headaches

(My daughter, who is now almost eight, suffered from headaches, nausea and earaches from the age of six and a half onwards. I took her to the GP who said that there was nothing wrong with her and, when we came back after a while because the symptoms weren't going away, indicated as much as that my daughter was just being naughty and that I was paying too much attention to her symptoms. I then took her to a homoeopath who gave her a course of tablets. Her condition improved, but this happened together with a considerable change in her lifestyle at that particular moment, as we spent the whole summer in Italy that year.

As soon as school started again, the symptoms returned and then even people at school were getting worried and told me that something ought to be done about her physical condition. They assured me that she didn't have any particular problems at school with her work or friends and that they didn't think she was pretending or seeking attention. We paid yet another visit to the GP and to an ear specialist, but on both occasions we were made to feel that we were being a nuisance.

Then I took her to someone who practised applied kinesiology. She diagnosed cranial distortion and scar tissue on the head, both caused by an accident when she was little, and also noticed a verruca on her foot, exactly on the spot of the kidney meridian. Both she and an osteopath started treating her and, since then, she has made immense progress. However, maybe most importantly, both my daughter and I felt an immense sense of relief that someone took us seriously, that, contrary to the findings of the GP and specialist, there was actually something physically wrong and that something could be done about it.

Since then we also discovered through a homoeopath that my daughter is extremely sensitive to chlorine. As she is a keen swimmer and swims two or three times a week, she is now taking tablets to counteract the reaction.)

Autism

(It wasn't until my son was about 14 months old that I began to suspect that something was wrong. Until then his development had been normal, although he had been plagued by ear, nose and throat infections which were treated with antibiotics and which the doctor didn't seem to think were unusual. By that time he was standing, had started talking and at 16 months he was walking, but something didn't feel right. As time went on he seemed withdrawn, stopped talking and became hyperactive and aggressive, with an unquenchable thirst and frequent urination and passing many loose stools per day. He developed obsessive habits and only rarely responded to us. Still, for a long time, I was the only one who felt there was something wrong with my son, with the result that one doctor told me I was neurotic.

When he was just about three years old, he had to be circumcised. At the time it seemed as if it tipped the balance, for he couldn't be reached at all in his pain and anger, even when he had physically recovered, and then his father also began to see something was wrong.

Just before he was four, the hospital ran many tests on him. Only a hearing loss showed up, with the result that grommets were fitted and his adenoids removed. As nothing else abnormal was detected, the doctors and psychologist felt he was either brain damaged or autistic and nothing medical would help him.

After yet another series of ear, nose and throat infections (again treated with antibiotics), I saw him deteriorate even further, with more obsessions, irrational fears, nightmares and bizarre behaviour. I had seen my baby develop normally, then change into this strange uncommunicative child, but I felt that he was in there somewhere, as confused as I was, and, if the doctors couldn't help him, then I had to find somebody who could, which is when I turned to alternative medicine.

First I tried diet and, after a period of trial and error, put him on the Feingold diet, modified to exclude all dairy products.

The first alternative practitioner we saw was a homoeopath, who concentrated on and cleared up the ear, nose and throat infections. She approved of the diet and recommended we try a cranial osteopath, which we did. He explained very carefully what he was doing and how he felt it would work. He felt my son wasn't brain damaged but autistic, and treated him for two years — first on a weekly basis, later once every two or three weeks — with a great deal of success.

Another treatment he has been having is biodynamic therapy — something I read about in a health magazine. This concentrates on the release of emotional tension. My son's relationship with his therapist there is a very special one, which in itself seems to have a healing effect. About a year ago I also started doing Tinbergen's holding therapy with him, which is particularly suitable for autistic children, and the best thing about this is that it is something I can do for him myself, rather than a therapist working with him. Lately we have also started to see a psychic healer regularly, which I feel is helping us on a different, more subtle level. The healer seems to complement all the other work that is going on, by shifting my son's energy and by promoting change inside him.

The progress my son has made during the past three years is considerable. From the mute, bizarre child previously described he has changed into a sociable, responsive and communicative boy. He is calmer and more independent, both physically and emotionally. He understands everything that is said to him and answers with signs and sometimes speaks. He sleeps well, his health is good, he is no longer doubly incontinent, and he is *fun*.

When we started our journey into alternative medicine, I wasn't sure what I was looking for or what to expect, but one therapy has led to another and I feel we are now left with therapies that work together, physically as well as emotionally. The approach from the alternative practitioners was totally different to what I had been used to (I used to work in the NHS), and I found this difficult to understand at first. However, it was very positive and supportive, and it has not only changed my son, but changed my attitude, making me understand myself and my son much better and helping us to see how we can help ourselves. 〉

Migraine

〈 If I tell you about my daughter, I should begin by saying that my daughter's father is a very experienced GP and that I have been involved in the Alexander technique for eight years, first by studying it, then by teaching. As a consequence I am very open to seeking help from both orthodox and complementary medical sources. I should also mention that my daughter was eight months old when her father and I separated.

My daughter had repeated ear infections for the first three years of her life, which were treated with antibiotics. When this began to worry me, I took her to a healer who worked with the feet and from whom I myself had received considerable benefit. The infections became much less severe, but she still constantly had a stuffed nose. I then took her to an (orthodox) allergy specialist who pronounced her allergic to house dust, which in our house, a permanent building site, was a drastic diagnosis. However, simple things like a foam mattress off the floor, washing the curtains often, polyester sheets, and foam pillows have made an enormous difference and she has very rarely needed antibiotics since.

Another problem has been her not getting to sleep until very late — she herself once said "What is between sleep and me?" — which still is not totally solved, although we are now working on it more successfully than we have for a long time. Through the referral of our GP we have been for a few sessions of family therapy and, although she only went once, I am still going myself. It seems to have a positive effect on her being willing to go to bed when she is tired, because the clearer I become through the counselling, the easier it is for both of us to handle our problems.

The major issue we have been dealing with for the last two years are frequent migraines. Several doctors said they would clear up with time, while it was also suggested that they were linked with the fact that when she was eight she didn't like school for the whole of that year. The migraines were so unpleasant that I had to take time off work, which caused financial hardship, and I then decided to take her to a cranial osteopath whose judgement I have proven trust in. He gave a mixed psychological and physical diagnosis and said that it was no wonder she was getting the migraines. Both my daughter and I were very relieved as people around us thought she was manufacturing them to get out of school and we both felt this was not true.

She has been having treatment for a year and a half now and, touch wood, she has stopped having migraines, although she gets mild headaches occasionally, which go away with paracetamol. The slow but steady cranial osteopathy has enabled me to understand much better which things upset my daughter and I have begun to allow her to express her feelings of sadness,

which before I was too frightened to do.

I think the combination of cranial osteopathy and the recent start of family therapy have shifted the migraine pattern and she is more confident and light-hearted that I have ever known her. Equally important in this whole process, I believe, is that I myself am having cranial osteopathy and counselling and am doing a lot of writing. Lately I have been giving myself permission to do the things I have always wanted and never allowed myself to do, and I am astounded by the positive effect all this is having on my daughter. I am particularly aware of the responsibility I have towards her as she enters puberty and in order to take it on joyfully, I have also begun to reassess my own feelings about being a woman. ❯

Coordination problems

❮ It all began with our second son having endless colds and coughs as a baby and being treated for them with lots of antibiotics. I myself was brought up on straight orthodox medicine and I had always used it for myself and the children, but when our second child was about one year old and had had the umpteenth course of antibiotics, I thought it was time to find out whether there were other ways of treating him.

I took him to a homoeopath, recommended to us by a friend, who treated him successfully for his colds. From then onwards I have used alternative medicine for my children more and more, although I also still use orthodox medicine from time to time. For instance, I had both

children vaccinated, but when the second one reacted badly to his last booster, the homoeopath gave him a remedy that helped him get over his symptoms.

My eldest child has never had as many colds and illnesses, but he had some other problems. A few years ago, when he was six and was finding reading difficult, it was discovered that he was not dominantly right- or left-handed, which was perhaps the cause of some of these problems. We went to see a practitioner of applied kinesiology who, among other things, gave us some right–left exercises to do at home. These exercises were very gentle and easy to do. Gradually his reading improved and within 18 months he was reading fluently. How much this improvement was due to the exercises or what would have occurred naturally is difficult to say.

More recently, we noticed that he was finding spelling difficult and that he was not progressing with certain physical activities such as swimming or football. I had just heard about educational kinesiology and from what I learnt about it, it seemed very appropriate for our son. I found someone who practised this new therapy and I took my son for a visit. During our first visit, the therapist immediately embarked on a set of vigorous exercises which, although on the whole seemed the type of exercises that would benefit my son, didn't seem to be particularly geared to his needs or frame of mind at that particular moment.

When we went away, my son was feeling all right but, later that day, problems started. He felt miserable, upset, and couldn't sleep, and I felt pretty sure his body was reacting to the treatment he had had earlier in the day. It seemed to me the exercises had "hit" the bits that needed help, but that it had all been too forceful. We didn't go back for further treatment, but we tried to do some of the exercises at home. Somehow they always seemed to make him edgy or distressed.

So, for the moment, we are not seeing any alternative practitioners. At school they have repeatedly assured me that my son is doing all right, which has made me wonder sometimes whether I am just worrying too much about him. ›

Glandular fever

‹ When she was eleven, my daughter came down with a high temperature, swollen glands and a headache. We thought it was glandular fever and so did the GP, although the blood test she was given turned out to be negative. The GP said there was nothing we could do about it, apart from bringing down the fever in the early stages, and that it usually took nine months to clear away. Then I took her to a homoeopathic doctor, who also diagnosed glandular fever. She gave her a course of treatment and after four weeks the symptoms disappeared and my daughter felt absolutely fine again. A year later, full recovery is still in evidence and no repeat visits either to the homoeopath or GP have been necessary for this specific illness. ›

Speech difficulties

‹ A boy of 13 came to see me at the community health project in a local hospital where I work. His mother brought him in because she was having shiatsu for her continuous headaches and they had cleared up. He had speech difficulties and had pains under his chest.

As I started taking a case history, his speech difficulties became immediately apparent. He was friendly and keen to communicate and would keep trying until he succeeded in getting across the point he was making, but the more embarrassed he became, the more problems he had producing the words. He had been having some speech therapy at school, but he said it hadn't helped much. It seemed to be a problem of production. There were no particular consonants that gave rise to the speech difficulties, but it had more to do with content and situation. The problem seemed to have started when he arrived in England and presumably began to learn English, but he said the problem was now just as bad in his first language. He mentioned that his older sister had also had a similar problem when she came to England, but she was better now.

The pain in his abdomen or under his chest had been checked by a doctor, who had found nothing particularly wrong. He was quite small and short for his age and his health otherwise appeared reasonable.

When I started treating him with shiatsu, I found that the energy in the heart meridian was very blocked. In Chinese medicine the heart energy controls the tongue. As I worked, he relaxed quite quickly and after the treatment the pain in his abdomen was gone, something about which he was clearly pleased. I explained to him that I thought the pain and the speech difficulties were related and that we could work on them together.

During his next session, apart from giving him shiatsu treatment, I also taught him some Japanese breathing exercises. The next time he came to see me he said he had been doing the exercises and he felt his speech was better. He also felt much better altogether. I couldn't honestly hear a difference, but if *he* felt his speech was better, this could be seen as a step in the right direction.

Over the next couple of months things gradually improved and we were both pleased with his progress. I have been treating him with shiatsu for seven months now. I have been working mostly with the heart energy, though sometimes the liver and gall bladder energy needs attention. We can't say there has been continuous improvement. There have been ups and downs that go with his fortunes both at school and in his wider family group. However, also as a result of the breathing exercises, I feel there has been a slow strengthening and calming of his energy and his speech has improved a great deal. He is now confident to speak to strangers and recently took part in a group discussion with adults and younger people. ⟩

Eczema

⟨ My son, who is now 16 years old, started to have trouble with his skin from the moment he was weaned at six months. Apart from causing eczema, any product made from cow's milk made him vomit. We then switched to goat's milk, which he could keep down, although it didn't help the eczema.

He was seen by at least five different doctors, none of whom seemed to be able to help him, and I then took him to the homoeopathic hospital. He spent one month there and they were very good at nursing him and treating him with creams that weren't harmful.

However, when he was one year old and still an out-patient at the homoeopathic hospital, his eczema continued to be pretty bad and it was decided that he was now old enough to have certain tests, which were to be carried out at Great Ormond Street Hospital for Sick Children. My son spent two months in the children's hospital, while four specialists looked after him and managed to sort his problems out. It became apparent that he suffered from multifarious allergies to many proteins and also to cat hairs and house dust. They put him on an elimination diet and gave him extra vitamins and soya milk, and soon he started to grow again, something he hadn't done for quite some time.

When I got him home, we were able to cope with his condition with the help of drugs and hydrocortisone creams, while sticking to a rigorous routine of keeping the house free of dust and cooking a special diet. His eczema came and went and came back again, and although we coped, he was obviously not a very healthy child.

When as a toddler he started going to a playgroup, one of the leaders noticed he was coughing a lot and she, being a homoeopath herself, offered to treat him. She managed to cure the cough, but didn't bring about much change in his skin condition.

When he was nine, a friend told me about an acupuncturist who had successfully treated him for hay fever and suggested that I should go with my son to see if it would improve his condition. We went and, immediately after the first session, which wasn't painless but lasted only four minutes, my son fell asleep in the car on our way back home. The second session took place a week later and was again very short if not painless, but my son, being used to all sorts of tests and treatments, was very brave about it. The following day his eczema started to clear and it then stayed away for a full year. At the children's hospital, where he was still being treated as an out-patient, they also noticed the improvement and were duly impressed with it.

After a year, however, his eczema returned, and we decided to go back to the same acupuncturist. This time he had ten treatment sessions, which unfortunately didn't manage to clear up his skin, although they had a beneficial effect on his runny nose and other sinus problems he had been having. By the way, I have, since then, discovered that acupuncture need not be painful at all if one goes to the right practitioner.

From that time onwards, his eczema has once again been something that comes and goes and which we have learned to cope with, although one of the side-effects of using hydrocortisone cream on his skin has been that his hands have turned quite rough and old-looking, rather an embarrassment to a boy who wants to be a guitarist. One of the periods when I felt he began to cope a lot better with his health problems as well as with the behavioural problems he was then having was when he took up martial arts for a while. It gave him the confidence and integration of body and mind he very much needed at the time. Also, he now notices that his eczema is worse during times of stress and that keeping physically fit through sports and exercise helps him to cope better with allergies and infections. **)**

Index